S0-CNE-693

INSIDE
the all-star game

A behind-the-scenes
look at the Midsummer Classic.

**MLB
INSIDERS
CLUB**

Baseball Insiders Library™

INSIDE
the all-star game

A behind-the-scenes
look at the Midsummer Classic.

MLB
INSIDERS
CLUB

Baseball Insiders Library™

INSIDE THE ALL-STAR GAME
A behind-the-scenes look at the Midsummer Classic.

Printed in 2011

CONTRIBUTORS' NOTE
Primary original reporting by Jon Schwartz and the editors of Major League Baseball.

ACKNOWLEDGEMENTS
Major League Baseball would like to thank Pat Kelly and Milo Stewart Jr. at the National Baseball Hall of Fame and Museum for their invaluable assistance, as well as Eric Enders, David Jones, Kristin Nieto and Craig Tomashoff for their diligent work in helping to prepare this book for publication.

A huge debt of gratitude also goes out to the employees of Major League Baseball and its clubs for being so generous with their time, and to the entire MLB public relations team for its monumental support along the way. All insights from these individuals were crucial to telling the story behind the Midsummer Classic.

MAJOR LEAGUE BASEBALL PROPERTIES
Vice President, Publishing
Donald S. Hintze

Editorial Director
Mike McCormick

Publications Art Director
Faith M. Rittenberg

Senior Production Manager
Claire Walsh

Associate Editor
Jon Schwartz

Associate Art Director
Melanie Finnern

Senior Publishing Coordinator
Anamika Panchoo

Project Assistant Editors
Allison Duffy, Chris Greenberg

Editorial Interns
Nicholas Carroll, Bill San Antonio

MAJOR LEAGUE BASEBALL PHOTOS
Director
Rich Pilling

Photo Editor
Jessica Foster

MLB INSIDERS CLUB
Managing Editor
Jen Weaverling

Art Director
Brian Peterson

Proofreader
Travis Bullinger

2 3 4 5 6 7 8 9 10 / 15 14 13 12 11

Copyright © MLB Insiders Club 2011

ISBN: 978-1-58159-531-4

All rights reserved. No part of this publication may be reproduced, stored in an electronic retrieval system or transmitted in any form or by any means (electronic, photocopying, recording or otherwise) without the prior or written permission of the copyright owner.

MLB Insiders Club
12301 Whitewater Drive
Minnetonka, MN 55343

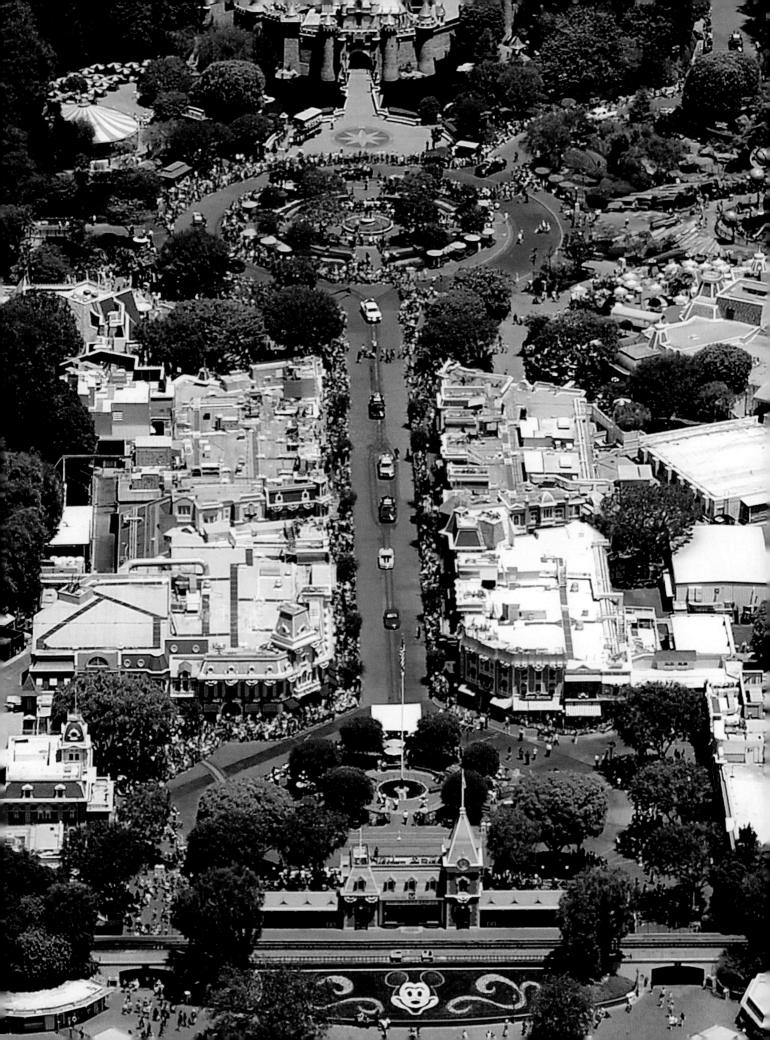

TABLE OF CONTENTS

INTRODUCTION

THERE'S AN INTERESTING THING ABOUT MAJOR LEAGUE BASEBALL'S SHOWCASE EVENTS: We all want our favorite team to make it to the World Series. But the All-Star Game is an event that we want to attend ourselves, maybe even more than we want our favorite players to go. Sure, we vote for our hometown heroes as part of the fan balloting and vociferously protest any perceived slight, but we would also be just as apt to trade a worthy player's All-Star trip for the chance to sit in the host park and witness the game in person.

Tickets are hard to come by. They *should* be hard to come by. Because there's nothing like Major League Baseball's Midsummer Classic. From the inaugural exhibition as part of the 1933 World's Fair to the extravagant spectacle we know and love today, the All-Star Game spotlights the top talent in the game on the biggest stage, with the largest audience of the summer. It's fun; it's entertaining; it's a party.

This is no knock on the World Series. Anything but. The World Series remains the pinnacle, the end of the line. The Fall Classic winners hoist a trophy that every All-Star would give anything to touch. But the seriousness of the last week in October is countered by the celebratory feel of the days leading up to the second Tuesday in July. Throughout the myriad events of All-Star Week, fans go wild for gopher balls and galas, circus catches and charitable causes, aces and autograph signings. Played by the same rules that govern a regular-season game or a winner-take-all playoff, the Midsummer Classic is the most intense All-Star affair in professional sports. It's about dominance, about the elite, about the best taking on the best. But most of all, it's about memories.

As fans, we remember the players. We remember the moments. But behind all of those memories are the hardworking people who spend their days and nights making these All-Star festivities worth remembering. From hanging banners throughout the host city to coordinating a presidential first pitch and a military flyover to laying down the red carpet, none of what makes the Midsummer Classic possible happens by itself. The excitement of All-Star Week is the fruit of years' worth of labor — from the All-Stars themselves down to those who ship their bats and gloves to the site of the game.

Even today, with the All-Star Game determining home-field advantage in the World Series, the result will really only impact two teams. But the individual moments — the sight of Hank Blalock rounding the bases in 2003 after solving the unsolvable Eric Gagne; of Hank Aaron, Willie Mays and Roberto Clemente lining up in the outfield for the National League during the 1960s; of Carl Hubbell striking out a string of Hall of Famers in 1934 — will live forever. Which is to say nothing of Josh Hamilton's 2008 Home Run Derby performance, or of the undeniable joy of watching up-and-coming stars like Evan Longoria and Alfonso Soriano for the first time in the All-Star Futures Game and then seeing them transform into superstars in the ensuing years.

As the pageantry of the Midsummer Classic grows each year, the potential for memories increases. Who knows how Babe Ruth might have fared if there had been a 1933 Home Run Derby? But perhaps that's the point. No matter how big All-Star Week gets, fans will still go crazy for any souvenir with the All-Star logo, thousands of media members will continue to descend on the city and all of that will become secondary once the best batters in the world step in to face the best pitchers — moments that will repeat throughout the night.

You'll want to be there for that.

CONSTELLATION When MLB's best gather each year for one night in July, it's a dazzling event.

CHAPTER 1: OPENING BID

A TREMENDOUS AMOUNT OF COORDINATION GOES INTO PLANNING BASEBALL'S midsummer celebration. Preparation begins as soon as the site is chosen, which is sometimes nearly two years before any tangible signs of the festivities appear in the host city. Before any banners can hang from buildings proclaiming the upcoming All-Star Week events, and certainly before lucky ticket holders can watch baseball's best in the marquee game itself, there are decisions to be made. The Commissioner of Baseball alone determines the game's location. He is responsible for sorting through the bids from teams jockeying for a slice of the Midsummer Classic each season. As the game has grown in popularity and All-Star Week has expanded to include beloved events such as the Home Run Derby and FanFest, the competition to host has grown fierce. Each year, Big League locales assemble impressive presentations in hopes of being tapped for the honor to be branded and transformed when the All-Star Game comes to town.

GRAND ENTRANCE Host cities herald the arrival of the All-Star Game, as New York did for the 2008 Midsummer Classic.

SPECIAL ANNOUNCEMENT
Commissioner Bud Selig
ultimately selects the host city
for the Midsummer Classic,
a distinction coveted by every
Major League team.

GETTING ORGANIZED

Whether the honor is used to reward a loyal fanbase or as an incentive toward building a new stadium, being chosen to host the Major League Baseball All-Star Game is a dream of every team and its supporters. The chance to host baseball's biggest party of the year, with the eyes of all sports-loving fans on your city, is about as good as it gets for a team — second only to hoisting the Commissioner's Trophy after winning the game's *other* main event in October.

In 2010, when Commissioner Bud Selig officially announced that Kansas City would host the 2012 Midsummer Classic, he estimated that the festivities could generate more than $70 million for the city, as visitors from all corners of the country would flock there to enjoy the spectacle. Beyond that, the many components of All-Star Week bring in significant funds for local charities. "The competition among our 30 clubs to play host to an All-Star Game has become incredibly intense in recent years," Commissioner Selig said. "All-Star Summer will give fans the opportunity to experience various celebrations of our game over a five- or six-day period in which fans will be able to reach out and touch our great game."

It wasn't always that easy for the Commissioner, who has the lone voice in selecting the host city each year. It used to be that he would have to ask teams to accept the game as a favor to him; now clubs line up for the chance — and once they're awarded Midsummer Classic hosting duties, they want to do it again soon after. Teams vying to host an All-Star Game aren't so different from countries jockeying to be the site of the Olympic Games; not only is it prestigious, but it also can be an economic boon for the city.

Teams that build new stadiums hope to eventually welcome the game, using it as a chance to showcase their ballpark and even, in some cases, to help alleviate the financial burden for its construction. In the case of the 2008 Midsummer Classic, the Yankees successfully bid for the game as a tribute to the history of Yankee Stadium, then in its final year. In Kansas City's case, the prospect of hosting the 2012 All-Star Game was a key factor in the city approving an extensive renovation of Kauffman Stadium, which first opened in 1973.

Of course, there's much more than just the ballpark to consider when designating a host city for the many events that currently compose All-Star Week.

"You have to think of the financial aspects — tickets, city services, hotels, convention center availability, transportation," said Marla Miller, Major League Baseball's senior vice president for special events. "There are inquiries from several cities [every year]."

The complex bid process involves securing approximately 3,000 hotel rooms per night for the duration of the long weekend, something that's easier to accomplish in July in Phoenix than New York; selecting a 400,000 square-foot convention space to house All-Star FanFest; devising transportation for shuttling players, VIPs and officials around the city; and envisioning ways that the city and the team can promote the event, both during and prior. Several teams submit bids, which are often not made known to the public, years ahead of time. The Commissioner's staff leaves nothing to chance, scouting out the host city's every last detail to ensure that the event can go off smoothly and provide an enjoyable experience for everyone from dignitaries and celebrities to lucky ticket holders.

The complex process requires years of commitment to planning and working on the event from the host club and MLB. And while the process is just beginning when Commissioner Selig announces his choice, it's a thrilling moment for a state, city and team.

"The people of Missouri are proud to showcase Kansas City and this beautiful stadium as we eagerly begin the countdown to 2012," Missouri Gov. Jay Nixon said in 2010.

A ROYAL CHOICE
Plans to upgrade Kauffman
Stadium depended upon the
Royals being tabbed to host the
All-Star Game in 2012.

LOGOS

THE LOGOS FOR EACH ALL-STAR GAME ARE USUALLY CREATED BY MLB'S IN-HOUSE DESIGN services department, occasionally in collaboration with a local artist, but that doesn't mean that the host team is left out of the process. Rather, the club is integral in the genesis of ideas, and the brainstorming begins when the team fills out a questionnaire that MLB distributes approximately two years before the event.

The hosts indicate which All-Star logos they have liked in the past, what colors they would like to see used, and how, in a general sense, they want their logo to look. After considering the team's responses, Anne Occi, MLB's vice president of design services, has her team get to work on developing logos to present to the host club. In the case of the Diamondbacks, hosts of the 2011 game, the eventual choice — and use of the color blue — wasn't what the club expected, but they were thrilled once they saw it. "I said, 'No, I'm not crazy about seeing blue,'" Diamondbacks President Derrick Hall told MLB.com of his thoughts before he saw the logo. But everything changed after he got a look for the first time. "It was an automatic yes, because it was the blue of our blue skies. I'm thrilled with the logo."

As part of the logo design, MLB actually creates an entire style guide unique to the event, with typesets and theme art that will become ubiquitous throughout the planning and during All-Star Week itself. The hope is that the designs in the style guide eventually create a subliminal reaction that allows a fan to recognize a specific typeset or color and associate it with the All-Star Game. The logo needs to look good blown up on the side of a building but also should not be so intricate that it can't be sewn easily onto a patch.

"The aim is to focus on iconography," Occi said. "You've seen bridge motifs in New York, the arch in St. Louis, things like that. It should be heritage driven, tradition driven."

Surprisingly, then, 2010 was the first time since 1995 that MLB used an actual star as the central element of the All-Star Game logo, tying the event itself in with the style of the Angels' logo — right down to the halo around the tip of the star.

THE INAUGURAL CLASSIC

It may surprise many baseball fans that the All-Star Game was never intended to be an annual event. As originally conceived by *Chicago Tribune* Sports Editor Arch Ward, it was supposed to be a one-off spectacle, a once-in-a-lifetime game that would bring more superstars together on the same field than any single event in history. Dubbed "The Game of the Century," it was MLB's contribution to the 1933 World's Fair in Chicago. The theme of the fair was "A Century of Progress" — a title applied as easily to Chicago, which was founded in 1833, as to baseball, which had existed in modern form since the 1830s.

The organizers of the World's Fair had already been looking for a grand sporting event to accompany the fair, so when Ward suggested a baseball All-Star Game, city fathers were ecstatic. Baseball executives, however, were less excited. In order to get the teams to participate, the *Tribune* had to agree to cover the cost of the game in the event that it lost money. Ward was so confident the game would be a success that he offered to put up the cash himself. In the months before the matchup, Ward made his case to each team owner, and one by one they agreed to participate. When the final holdout — the Boston Braves — gave its approval in late May, the contest was officially scheduled for July 6.

Ward quickly set about organizing a voting system by which fans could elect players, although each league's manager retained final veto power over the lineup. With the help of their local sports editors, fans across the nation mailed in their votes, and the *Tribune* tallied the ballots. With most of the votes coming from Chicago, the leading vote-getter was not Babe Ruth, but instead White Sox outfielder Al Simmons, who was batting .368 that season. The players, already enthusiastic about participating, were even more delighted when it was announced that proceeds from the game would benefit the National Association of Professional Baseball Players, which offered charitable help to indigent former ballplayers. The best seats

in the house would cost $1.65, but fans could gain admission to the bleachers for just 55 cents.

The tickets, of course, sold out quickly. Fans showed up well before the 1:15 p.m. starting time to watch the teams take batting practice, and players reveled in the opportunity to converse with each other as teammates rather than opponents. "During the early preliminaries the great crowd could not have found itself more occupied had a nine-ringed circus been in progress," *The New York Times* noted. "One of the warmest receptions of the day was tendered to Lefty Grove … but the greatest ovation of all seemed to go to [Carl] Hubbell as the Giant left-hander started tuning up his mighty arm that pitched eighteen scoreless innings last Sunday."

The American League lineup, virtually everyone agreed, was the greatest assembled in the history of baseball to that point. Seven of the nine starters would eventually be elected to the Hall of Fame, including Ruth and Lou Gehrig. The lineup was so strong, in fact, that Jimmie Foxx — who went on to win the AL Triple Crown that year — was forced to ride the pine. With such a star-studded batting order, it was ironic that the first run in All-Star history was driven in by pitcher Lefty Gomez, whose .144 career average was terrible even by hurlers' standards of the day. With two outs in the top of the second, Gomez knocked a single to center to score Jimmy Dykes, and the Junior Circuit never looked back. They would win, 4-2.

An inning later, the fans got the moment they had been waiting for when Ruth smashed a two-run homer that landed just fair in the right-field stands. By the time Grove struck out pinch-hitter Tony Cuccinello to end the game, it was clear that the event had been even more successful than anyone hoped. Even irascible NL Manager John McGraw, in a rare display of sportsmanship, made his way over to the AL clubhouse to congratulate the victors. "Hello, John," AL skipper Connie Mack said. "Wasn't it swell?"

PITCH IN

Although the first officially sanctioned All-Star Game wasn't played until 1933, the idea arguably took root as early as 1911, when American League players banded together to mourn the death of a beloved star. Cleveland pitcher Addie Joss, who still owns the second-best career ERA in MLB history at 1.89, passed away in April 1911 at age 31, a victim of meningitis. Joss's widow and children were left without any means of support, so his Naps teammates organized a benefit that pitted the club against stars from the other seven AL teams. The ever-gruff Ty Cobb enthusiastically agreed to travel to Cleveland for the game, as did six other future Hall of Famers. They dubbed their team the "All-Stars," one of the first times that term had been used in baseball. Behind three innings of one-hit relief from Walter Johnson, plus two hits apiece by Cobb, Tris Speaker and Eddie Collins, the All-Stars defeated Cleveland, 5-3. The real winners, though, were Lillian Joss and her two young children, who received a check for $12,914.

MIDSUMMER TRUCE
Rival skippers Connie Mack
(left) and John McGraw
smiled for the cameras at
the 1933 All-Star Game.

ACES WILD Carl Hubbell (left) and Lefty Grove were among the future Hall of Famers who took the field in the 1933 All-Star Game.

INSTANT HIT

SAFE BET
Josh Gibson slides home safely during the 1944 East-West Game at Comiskey Park in Chicago.

THE INAUGURAL MLB ALL-STAR GAME IN 1933, OF COURSE, DIDN'T feature *all* of the sport's stars — Josh Gibson, Oscar Charleston, Willie Wells and other great African-American players were nowhere to be found on the field. But Negro Leagues promoters knew a good idea when they saw one. Within three months of MLB's first Midsummer Classic, the Negro Leagues had created an All-Star Game of its own, dubbed the East-West Game.

"One particular day we were sitting in a restaurant in Pittsburgh," recalled former Chicago American Giants Manager Dave Malarcher before his death in 1982. "And [Pittsburgh Crawfords Secretary Roy Sparrow] said, 'You know, Dave, we could organize a big game like the Major League All-Star Game and call it the East-West Game.' About three weeks later when we came to Chicago, we found that … they had organized the first East-West Game. They picked the best of the players from the East and the best of the players from the West, and they rented Comiskey Park."

The rental terms stipulated that the game's organizers pay 20 percent of the annual proceeds from the contest to the White Sox for use of their stadium, but there were plenty of profits to go around. Indeed, the East-West Game became such a popular event that it drew a *larger* audience than the Major League All-Star Game nine times in its first 18 years of existence. African-American fans planned vacations to coincide with the game, while special trains came to Chicago from points east and south for the festivities.

The inaugural contest in 1933 was thrilling, with 18 total runs scored, but it was the 1934 East-West Game that became an unforgettable classic. With the game tied, 0-0, in the eighth, speedster Cool Papa Bell, then a member of the Kansas City Monarchs, won it for the East with his legendary legs. Bell walked, stole second and scored the game's first run from second base on an infield hit. Gibson dazzled offensively, too — as he would do for 12 career East-West Games, including the 1944 contest, when he was 2 for 3 with a double and run scored — but that lone run was all that was needed. Thanks to the efforts of winning pitcher Satchel Paige of the Pittsburgh Crawfords, who whiffed five batters in four innings of two-hit relief, the West remained scoreless. "No greater pitcher ever performed at Comiskey Park than did the Satchel Paige of Sunday," the *Pittsburgh Courier* proclaimed.

The East-West Game became such a popular event that it drew a larger audience than the Major League All-Star Game nine times in its first 18 years of existence. Special trains came to Chicago for the festivities.

DRESSING THE CITY

THERE'S NO QUESTION THAT THE WORLD SERIES IS THE MOST dramatic event on the baseball calendar, the culmination of another season with a champion crowned. But with the structure of the play-offs, no one knows for sure which teams will be in the Fall Classic until a few days before the first pitch is thrown. The result is an event that takes place almost entirely inside the ballpark, with little visible evidence of the Series present in other areas of the city, aside from the swell of civic pride and a greater number of baseball caps.

That is decidedly *not* the case when it comes to the All-Star Game. With years to plan a design scheme, MLB's design services department turns the host city into its own artistic canvas, spreading the event's spirit well beyond stadium gates. Creating everything from small-scale invitations for various All-Star celebrations to gigantic banners hung on city buildings, MLB seeks local businesses to assist with the process. Design Services VP Anne Occi begins meeting with these vendors about 11 months before the game. "You want to make an impact when you go into a new city, and local businesses are enthusiastic to get involved in such a storied event," Occi said.

Occi's group also contacts city or county planners and chambers of commerce to find out what they'll be able to do around the city and for how long. Answers vary depending on the location. Along New York's gridded streets, streetlight banners and ads on public telephones were everywhere; in a more suburban area, the possibilities are different. In Anaheim, for example, Occi's team stretched banners across streets, hanging them from palm trees along Convention Way, the site of the MLB hotels and All-Star FanFest.

MLB's design team treats the whole city that way, scouting it out, taking thousands of photos, then creating renderings and going over them with city planners. In San Francisco, the center anchorage of the Bay Bridge provided a great spot to project an All-Star Game logo, which required a barge to be positioned in the bay. In Pittsburgh, banners were suspended inside the towers of the Roberto Clemente Bridge. The use of banners began in Chicago in 2003, when MLB hung All-Star bunting along highway overpasses.

Each host team has a liaison who works with MLB's design services team throughout the planning process. The liaison begins scouting during the previous All-Star Game, observing the event from all angles and to get a feel for what can be done, then helping to figure out methods to bring that sensibility to their own city. "You want to get to know the city so that you know where people are likely to be taking pictures. You want to make those areas great," Occi said. "You're doing this *for* the city, not *to* the city, and for the locals and tourists alike."

Installation of banners and signs begins about six weeks prior to the game, starting at airports. Huge ads appear, with All-Star Game logos and tune-in messages abounding. Four weeks out, street banners pop up. MLB aims for 500–800 around the city, depending on the size and nature of the location. Lastly, within two weeks of the game, hotels and other buildings hang massive signs. In San Francisco, City Hall was illuminated with the All-Star colors, and in New York in 2008, the Empire State Building was lit up for the contest.

And it's not just MLB's internal team that gets the fever. For the 2005 game in Detroit, General Motors placed ads that could be seen from inside Comerica Park on buildings in the surrounding area. To promote the Home Run Derby, they featured the gigantic image of a baseball crashing through a window of the city's iconic Renaissance Center, including a distance marker from home plate.

"You want to make everything feel big and have energy," Occi said. "You're making a memory. You want to have enough decorations around the city to help get the event engraved into everyone's memory."

STATUES

IN 2003, WHEN THE BASEBALL BOBBLEHEAD CRAZE PEAKED, MLB got in on the fun during All-Star Week, placing six-foot tall bobblehead statues throughout Chicago. The tradition has continued every year since 2008. In 2010, MLB teamed with Disney and licensee Forever Collectibles to place 36 Mickey Mouse statues — each 7.5 feet tall and weighing nearly 1,000 pounds — around Southern California. Similarly, MLB brought team-designed Statue of Liberty replicas to New York in 2008 and placed themed Gateway Arch replicas around St. Louis in '09. Each was a popular tourist attraction, and smaller versions of the statues are sought-after collector's items. "By selecting a statue design that represents a well-known aspect of the host city — like the Arch in St. Louis and Mickey Mouse in Anaheim — we hope to create a feeling that something big is happening in the city," said Howard Smith, senior vice president, licensing, for MLB. "It's a fun way for fans to get in the All-Star spirit and is a souvenir for that year's event."

BANNER DAY
A towering sign on Pittsburgh's Roberto
Clemente Bridge heralded the '06 event.

CHAPTER 1: OPENING BID

STREET VIEW
San Francisco's All-Star trolleys made sure that everyone knew that the '07 game was in town.

ARCH RIVALS
Replicas of St. Louis's famed Gateway
Arch touted the 2009 contest.

STATUESQUE
All-Star Game–themed Statue of Liberty replicas welcomed fans to New York in 2008.

WESTWARD HO!
A cowboy boot in Houston at
the '04 All-Star Game pointed the
way toward the eventual 2007 site.

MAGIC KINGDOM
Fans of all ages couldn't help but smile when the All-Star Game came to Anaheim in 2010.

TICKET HUB
Tickets to the 2008 All-Star Game in New York included dirt from Yankee Stadium.

TICKETING

I**T'S LIKE THE** C**ARNEGIE** H**ALL JOKE**. H**OW DO YOU GET TO THE** A**LL-**S**TAR** G**AME**? L**OTS OF** batting practice. For the rest of us, though, it's about snagging one of the prized ducats. The job of getting those tickets to fans falls on Rob Capilli, MLB's director of special events.

Capilli's job gets underway about a year before All-Star Week, when he begins pricing all seating sections at the stadium and setting the allotments for season ticket holders and MLB. As demand for All-Star Game tickets has grown over the years, prices have increased. Ticket prices are usually set in November and actually cost more than World Series passes. "People know that the World Series could come back to their city next year," Capilli said. "But they know that the All-Star Game is a once-in-a-lifetime experience that will not be back for at least another 20 years or so." In a typical year, season ticket holders receive a kit in April with information about buying strips of seats. A strip includes tickets for all of the All-Star events from Sunday through Tuesday, access into FanFest and a *Limited Edition Official All-Star Game Program*. At the same time, Capilli finishes allocating strips to the All-Stars themselves, with each player getting six tickets, along with the players' union, the Commissioner's Office, the other 29 clubs, the umpires, scouts and other relevant participants. Once season ticket holders have had their chance to purchase strips, a public opportunity for the right to buy the remaining inventory is held. The amount released to the public varies, but limited quantities mean it's a tough ticket.

The tickets are printed at Weldon, Williams & Lick (WWL) in Fort Smith, Ark. WWL is a leader in the ticket-printing business, also printing ducats for major events like the Super Bowl — and that's no small point in an industry that works so hard to make its tickets impossible to counterfeit. It's necessary to use a printer with a good reputation and good security to ensure that the printing plates don't get out to the public and that the security features on the tickets are as advanced as possible.

Once the events begin, Capilli's team has already been on-site for almost a week, setting up the Commissioner's on-field box and suite and the satellite ticket office in the MLB staff hotel. Clients pick up tickets, and Capilli shuffles his attention between troubleshooting at the ballpark, FanFest and the hotel.

CHAPTER 2: GETTING THERE

ASSEMBLING AN EVENT OF ALL-STAR PROPORTIONS IS QUITE A PROCESS. IT takes the diligent work of those on and off the field to make sure that baseball's marquee summer contest goes off without a hitch. There are votes to be cast, ballots to be counted and more than 70 players to be notified and ferried to the host city. Marketing campaigns must be coordinated by MLB and its broadcast partners, and uniforms must be assembled — sometimes moments before the first pitch, as final roster tweaks are often made at the 11th hour. None of it happens by accident. Both players and fans must do their part to ensure that the best first-half performances are rewarded with a spot in the All-Star cast. This build-up includes Joe DiMaggio's 48-game hitting streak that ushered him into the 1941 game. It's Ted Williams blazing into his first Midsummer Classic with a .405 average. It's a surge of fan support to make sure that an eventual league MVP isn't left off the roster. And all of the coordination is worth it when the All-Stars take the field.

TOP IT ALL OFF Once a player snags his very own All-Star gear, he can be confident that he ranks among the game's elite.

MAKING THE TEAM

THE MIDSUMMER CLASSIC IS AN ANNUAL CELEBRATION OF baseball, a long week full of pageantry and positive energy as the sport recognizes the best of the best.

Of course, none of that would be possible without choosing the 34 All-Stars from each league to take the field, and the process of selecting them begins with the fan ballot. Voting takes place in all 30 Major League stadiums and about 100 Minor League ballparks with a ballot sponsored by Firestone, at Lowe's Home Improvement stores with a ballot sponsored by Scotts and online at MLB.com. In 2010, fans cast a combined 21.2 million votes. Polls open just a few weeks after Opening Day.

Fans have selected the game's starters since 1947 — with the exception of a break from 1958–69 after a controversial 1957 vote. Just one player from each offensive position is on the ballot from each team, aside from the outfield slots; all outfielders are grouped into one pool. The AL ballot also includes one designated hitter per team. Once the ballot is finalized, it is unveiled at the ballpark that's slated to host that year's Midsummer Classic, and fan voting begins. Each team's in-stadium voting extends through approximately 22 home dates. Although the exact number of games differs each year, each club gets an equal amount.

"Every year, millions of fans participate in one of the greatest traditions in sports," said Tim Brosnan, MLB's executive vice president, business. "Thanks to the support of our partners both in the United States and abroad, baseball fans around the world can cast votes for their favorite players as part of the largest balloting program in sports."

After each homestand, clubs send the ballots they have collected to an independent entity that has been counting MLB's All-Star ballots for more than 20 years. There, votes from stadiums and Lowe's stores are tallied, and the results are compiled. Results are sent to MLB's offices, and, starting after Memorial Day, weekly updates are sent out in press releases. Balloting concludes in late June. But that's just the start of it.

Concurrently with fan voting, players do their part to recognize their peers. Since 2003, players have been voting for those they believe deserve to be All-Stars, and it's not a job that they take lightly. "It's as serious as it gets," Braves catcher Brian McCann said during

2010 All-Star Week. "If you don't take it seriously, then I just think this doesn't mean anything. The best players deserve to be here."

Each team's player representative works with the club's public relations department to help coordinate the process, which entails players voting by secret ballot in mid-June. Like the fans, Major Leaguers select one player for each offensive position, but they also choose five starting pitchers and three relievers. The ballots are printed in English and Spanish, and while there's never 100 percent participation because of injuries — although ballots are sent to injured players on rehab assignments — and other distractions, the numbers are representative. Each player secures his secret ballot in an envelope with his signature across the seal to ensure that it's not tampered with.

Once all of the ballots are collected and sent to MLB, eight to 10 auditors from Ernst & Young come to MLB's New York office to tabulate the votes. The top vote-getters at each position in the player balloting are selected to the team. If the players choose the same winner as the fans, the second-place finisher on the player ballot gets the nod.

Next, both All-Star managers — an honor bestowed upon each league's pennant-winning skipper from the previous year — round out the rosters with their selections. It's the managers' responsibility to make sure that each of the 30 clubs is represented, which can sometimes cut into the number of choices that they get to make on their own. The managers are also tasked with assembling a pitching staff that's at least 13 hurlers deep.

Most All-Star managers consult with skippers around the league to compare thoughts on which players belong, as well as to find out who will and will not be available for the game due to injury or workload. Managers also consult their own coaching staffs as they try to put together the best possible roster. As far as allegiance to their players goes, some managers fear the perception that they're just looking to reward their own guys, while others — knowing that, at the end of the day, their greatest responsibility is to their own team — don't hesitate to scoop up members of their squad.

"I always felt it was much more of an honor — not that the fans shouldn't have the vote — to be picked by your peers to be a part of

REGISTERED VOTER
All-Star Brian McCann
takes pride in the player
ballots he submits every year.

the All-Star Team," said nine-time All-Star Goose Gossage. "Whether the All-Star manager and coaches or the managers around the league picked you or helped the manager that was managing that year pick the team, I always felt it was a great honor that I was a part of those teams because of being chosen by the guys in charge. Not that I take away anything from the fans having the vote — I think it's exciting for them — but sometimes it becomes kind of a popularity contest."

Once the managers' picks are set, the teams are announced during the highly anticipated MLB All-Star Game *Selection Show*, which airs on TBS. The uninitiated might think this show concludes the process, but it's really just gaining steam. Whether because of injuries or because of the rule stipulating that pitchers who throw in a game on Sunday before the All-Star Game are ineligible to pitch in the Midsummer Classic, late tweaks to the All-Star rosters happen yearly.

By the first pitch of the Midsummer Classic, no one remembers whether a player was voted in originally or was added as a roster replacement in the days leading up to the contest. Regardless, he's an All-Star, a title that will stay with him for the rest of his career.

"It's a great feeling," relief pitcher Matt Capps said after being named the Washington Nationals' 2010 representative. "They called me into the office Sunday morning and told me I had been selected to the team. That was the last thing I thought of or had any idea about until General Manager Mike Rizzo told me. So, kind of the element of surprise and I didn't know what to expect — they were all sitting there and told me, and they all smiled and got all excited, and I was the same way. So, it was a fun experience for me."

BALLOT STUFFING

While the unpredictability of sports proves the saying about games not being played *on* paper, the 1957 All-Star Game illustrated that games can be played *with* paper. Once fan votes were tallied for the All-Star Game in St. Louis, seven Reds found themselves in the starting lineup after a Cincinnati newspaper distributed pre-marked ballots. Even Reds outfielder Wally Post, who would finish the season with a .244 average, edged out future Hall of Famers Hank Aaron and Willie Mays. To the delight of fans in the host city, Cardinals first baseman Stan Musial was the only non-Reds player voted an NL starter. Sensing that something was amiss, Commissioner Ford Frick substituted Mays and Aaron for Reds Gus Bell and Post, and fan voting was put on hold from 1958–69.

Once the controversy was settled, the game was a cracker. Leading, 3-2, after eight, the AL racked up three runs in the ninth. Even trailing, 6-2, the NL was not about to go quietly. Musial led off the bottom of the inning with a walk and scored on a Mays triple. An RBI single from Ernie Banks pulled the NL within a run. With two outs and the tying run in scoring position, pinch-hitter Gil Hodges dug into the batter's box for his last career All-Star at-bat. Hodges laced a shot to left-center, and the ball looked like it might get through. But outfielder Minnie Minoso came sprinting into view to snag the liner and preserve the victory for the AL.

THE LUCKY ONE
Reliever Matt Capps was the Washington Nationals' sole representative at the 2010 All-Star Game in Anaheim.

FINAL VOTE

THE LAST STEP IN SELECTING ALL-STAR ROSTERS IS THE FINAL Vote, in which fans go online to MLB.com to vote for one of five players from each league to round out the rosters. The All-Star managers select the candidates, and voting lasts for four days.

The 2010 Final Vote was particularly noteworthy, as fans rallied en masse to get eventual NL MVP Joey Votto added to the All-Star roster. He led all Final Vote contestants with 13.7 million tallies, as fans corrected what they saw as the ultimate snub — Votto failing to be selected in the fan and player votes. On the AL side, the Yankees'

Nick Swisher narrowly prevailed over Kevin Youkilis of the Red Sox in the closest race since the Final Vote began in 2002. Overall, more than 250 million votes were cast in the first nine years.

Creative get-out-the-vote campaigns are a part of the Final Vote. In May 2006, White Sox catcher A.J. Pierzynski, who had famously brawled with Cubs catcher Michael Barrett earlier in the year, was an AL candidate. Barrett punched Pierzynski in the face — and unwittingly began the process that would send his rival to the All-Star Game. The White Sox's slogan that year was simple: Punch A.J.

MARKETING CAMPAIGN

DEREK JETER IS MANNING HIS POSITION BETWEEN SECOND and third when Fox broadcaster Joe Buck's voice rises in the background. Suddenly, sand starts sweeping across Jeter's feet. Quick cut to Philly, where Ryan Howard and Jimmy Rollins try to make sense of the sand falling from the dugout roof. Images flash, from Matt Holliday's bat to Boston's Green Monster and finally to the wall at Safeco Field as a diving Ichiro Suzuki breaks through the baseball world onto a Southern California beach. There baseball's biggest stars, from Alex Rodriguez to Tim Lincecum, are enjoying some fun in the sun, while a giant sandcastle version of Angel Stadium rises from the shore and a modern rendition of the classic beach pop tune "California Sun" plays.

Fox Sports' tune-in ads for the 2010 All-Star Game hit all the right notes. The game's elite players? Check. An upbeat celebratory vibe bound to attract fans? Of course. But most importantly, they focused on the distinctive, local feel that makes each MLB All-Star Game unique.

"We want a campaign that celebrates the stars of the game and the feel of the host city," said Jacqueline Parkes, MLB's chief marketing officer. "By featuring the best players in the game with the unique qualities of the city, we hope the ads will resonate with viewers that this year's All-Star Game is a must watch."

Fox Sports' tune-in ads for the 2010 All-Star Game hit all the right notes. Most importantly, they focused on the distinctive, local feel that makes each MLB All-Star Game unique.

The 2010 ads — which were televised for about a month before the contest, mostly during MLB games or other sports broadcasts — conformed to the recent tradition of touting the sport's stars and the host city. In '09, ads showed players and fans being magnetically drawn to St. Louis's arch, which traveled the country before its final stop in Busch Stadium. For the '08 All-Star Game, the last one held at the old Yankee Stadium, the ballpark's famed bridge frieze spread throughout the city in ads interspersed with images of A-Rod and Albert Pujols.

Fox works with Parkes to develop creative elements for the ads, which are usually shot during Spring Training. Working with award-winning visual effects studio The Mill in 2010, Fox's design team seamlessly tied the sport into the overall look and feel of a SoCal summer.

The ad blitz is strongest in the home city, where MLB also runs print, TV and radio ads for FanFest and other All-Star events. Fox produces custom local ads, often featuring stars from that city who are featured on the All-Star ballot. In Tampa, for example, fans watching Rays games from the couch or at Tropicana Field might have seen All-Star ads centered on local stars David Price or Evan Longoria. All MLB broadcasts in the weeks leading up to the All-Star festivities also include drop-in ads, with announcers promoting the Midsummer Classic during breaks in action.

ALL-STARS AMONG US

THE ODDS AGAINST BECOMING AN ALL-STAR ARE ASTRONOMICAL, hard to conceive even for the world's greatest dreamers. But as Major League Baseball and *People* magazine have proven, anyone can be an All-Star in the community. In 2009, MLB and *People* launched the "All-Stars Among Us" campaign to recognize everyday heroes from all 30 clubs' fanbases. Since then, fans have been able to nominate and vote for regular citizens who do extraordinary things in their communities, and before the 2009 and 2010 All-Star Games, the winners — representing each of the 30 clubs — were honored in an on-field ceremony. From that group, one community All-Star was chosen to be featured in a July issue of the magazine.

"We are thrilled to partner with MLB to shine a spotlight on the inspiring work of these 'All-Stars Among Us,' and to salute these individuals in front of a nationwide audience," said Paul Caine, then Time Inc.'s style & entertainment group president. In total, the 2010 program received more than 1.7 million votes.

"I think those guys do better than we do," said Brewers All-Star outfielder Corey Hart. "We do what we do because, obviously, we love baseball, but you can't say enough for the guys that go out there and do the things that are going to be there tomorrow — the charity work they do. They find a way to be special to somebody, and I think we as players look up to those guys more than they look up to us."

In the weeks prior to the All-Star Game, each team recognizes its finalists with pregame ceremonies, when they throw ceremonial first pitches and are feted on the field, often getting the opportunity to mingle with players, as well. Additionally, Major League Baseball produces a booklet featuring the 30 winners that is distributed to all fans who attend the All-Star Game.

In 2010, Ruthe Rosen was chosen to represent the host Los Angeles Angels. She created and co-founded the Let It Be Foundation in 2006 to honor her daughter, who died of an inoperable brain tumor. Rosen's organization helps children in Southern California who are battling life-threatening illnesses. It also supports their families in maintaining a sense of normalcy in their lives, assisting them with housekeeping, grocery shopping and family recreation. "Humbling is an understatement," Rosen said during All-Star Week. "If I can continue to inspire other people that are having tough times and take their life lessons and do something incredible with it, that is the biggest thing."

"Hopefully this well-deserved recognition that our 'All-Stars Among Us' will receive from this event will make a significant impact on all of these organizations and their efforts to help other human beings," said Commissioner Bud Selig. "I want to thank *People* magazine for their partnership in this effort, but most importantly, I want to thank all of the 'All-Stars Among Us' for all that you've done. I'm really very proud on behalf of Major League Baseball to meet all of you and to celebrate your absolutely remarkable achievements."

STARRY NIGHT The 30 "All-Stars Among Us" took the field with players at Angel Stadium in 2010.

STAR OF STARS

SULTAN OF SUMMER
Babe Ruth (right) wowed
in the inaugural All-Star
Game in Chicago in 1933.

SEEING LEGENDARY NEW YORK YANKEES SLUGGER BABE RUTH IN action at the 1933 All-Star Game was a thrill not only for the fans, but also for a great many players. In those days, before Interleague Play and organized Spring Training, there were "National League veterans who have never seen Babe Ruth swing at a ball," John Kieran noted in *The New York Times*.

As his impressive but not otherworldly .312 average and 18 homers at the All-Star break attested, the 38-year-old Bambino was slowing down by the inaugural matchup in 1933 — but there was no question that baseball's greatest icon would bat third in the American League lineup. Al Simmons of the hometown White Sox may have been the AL's leading vote-getter, but Ruth was the man people wanted to see. "He is getting along in years," Kieran wrote. "He is a bit slow in the field. A fast ball gets by him now and then. But give him a crowd, a gallery worthy of his best effort, and the old warrior will put on a show." And put on a show he did.

NL southpaw Bill Hallahan, who had struck out the Babe earlier in the game, tried to sneak a fastball past him in the third inning. Like many others who had tried that before, Hallahan could only turn and watch as Ruth's line drive landed just inside the right-field foul pole. It was the first home run in All-Star Game history, and it earned Ruth a standing ovation from the nearly 50,000 fans at Comiskey Park who were accustomed to jeering him. Ruth was a star on defense, too, robbing an extra-base hit at the wall in the eighth.

Ruth's second and final All-Star Game in 1934 was equally memorable, albeit for a different reason. It was the first time that New York's greatest hitter faced its greatest pitcher — Giants ace Carl Hubbell. On his way to fanning five batters in a row, Hubbell unleashed his specialty, a screwball on the outside corner, and the Babe took it for a called strike three.

MOWING 'EM DOWN

The second-ever All-Star Game, in 1934, featured one of the biggest offensive explosions of any Midsummer Classic — 16 runs — but it was Carl Hubbell's dominant pitching performance that went down in history. Hubbell, a lanky left-hander for the New York Giants, was in the middle of the second of what would be five consecutive 20-win seasons and had won the NL MVP Award in 1933. Pitching against an American League lineup in which all nine starters were future Hall of Famers, Hubbell thrilled his hometown fans at the Polo Grounds by striking out five of those awesome sluggers in a row: Babe Ruth, Lou Gehrig, Jimmie Foxx, Al Simmons and Joe Cronin. The quintet would combine for 140 homers and 584 RBI that season, but they were no match for Hubbell's patented screwball. Said a befuddled Cronin after the game: "Hubbell is unquestionably the greatest pitcher I have ever seen."

FIRST-HALF DOMINANCE

WHEN IT COMES TIME TO CHOOSE THE ALL-STAR TEAMS EACH SUMMER, NO ONE CAN predict what a player's statline is going to look like once the season concludes. Some players, though, put up first halves so dominant, they could have stopped right then.

1941 Joe DiMaggio: .357 AVG, .434 OBP, .650 SLG, 19 HR, 71 RBI, 72 R

At just 26 years old, Joe DiMaggio arrived in Detroit for the 1941 All-Star Game as the most popular man in the country and the most revered American athlete since Babe Ruth. For the previous two weeks, the New York Yankees center fielder had dominated the sport's headlines as his epic hitting streak shattered record after record. By the All-Star break, DiMaggio's string stood at an unprecedented 48 games. Even Boston's Ted Williams, who entered the break with a .405 average, was impressed. "I really wish I could hit like that guy Joe DiMaggio," he said.

1947 Larry Doby: .414 AVG, 14 HR

In July 1947, Indians Owner Bill Veeck acquired Larry Doby, then a 23-year-old second baseman for the Newark Eagles of the Negro National League, for $10,000. Newark Owner Effa Manley reluctantly accepted the offer for her star player, and told Veeck, "You know, if Larry Doby were white and a free agent, you'd give him $100,000 to sign as a bonus."

Manley's praise was not misplaced. Doby became the American League's first black player after a dazzling first half for the Eagles. The following year, Doby would help lead the Indians to their second — and most recent — championship by batting .318 in the 1948 World Series.

1971 Vida Blue: 17-3, 1.42 ERA, 188 K, 184.1 IP

With a fastball clocked in the upper 90s and a devastating curve, 21-year-old left-handed pitcher Vida Blue took the baseball world by storm in the opening months of the 1971 season. He won 17 of his first 22 starts for the Athletics, inviting comparisons to Dodgers Hall of Famer Sandy Koufax, who thought the analogy a mismatch. "I couldn't get the ball over the way he does at [that] age," Koufax explained. "He's not only ahead of me, he's ahead of the world."

By the All-Star break, Blue had pushed the A's to a surprising 11.5-game lead in the AL West standings, and he was on pace to finish the season with 32 wins and 350 strikeouts.

1975 Joe Morgan: .345 AVG, .487 OBP, .547 SLG, 13 HR, 60 RBI, 61 R

Heading into the 1975 All-Star break, Cincinnati Reds second baseman Joe Morgan led the league in on-base percentage, stolen bases (40) and walks (80); ranked second in batting average and runs scored; and was fourth in RBI. All the while, he played Gold Glove–caliber defense and powered the Reds to a 61-29 record, 12.5 games ahead of the second-place Los Angeles Dodgers in the NL West.

By the 1941 All-Star break, DiMaggio's string stood at an unprecedented 48 games. Even Boston's Ted Williams, who entered the break with a .405 average, was impressed. "I really wish I could hit like that guy Joe DiMaggio," he said.

HOME-FIELD ADVANTAGE

ONCE UPON A TIME, THE THOUGHT OF TREATING THE ALL-STAR GAME LIKE A FRIENDLY exhibition was anathema. Baseball's all-time Hits King Pete Rose embodied the competitive spirit of his day. "Pete was into it," said Hall of Famer and 11-time NL All-Star Gary Carter. "He would get up in the clubhouse before the game and would be his boisterous self and say: 'Come on, let's go! Let's get fired up!' He really wanted to beat the American League."

As the years passed, though, increased player movement between the leagues engendered a more genial atmosphere. After the 2002 game ended in a tie when both teams ran out of pitchers in extra innings, Commissioner Bud Selig felt that the Midsummer Classic needed a boost, instituting a rule awarding home-field advantage in the World Series to the league that wins the All-Star Game.

The 2003 Midsummer Classic at Chicago's U.S. Cellular Field was the first with more than pride on the line. Promoted with the tagline "This Time It Counts," the game delivered. Hank Blalock, a 22-year-old representing the Rangers, knocked an Eric Gagne fastball over the wall in the eighth to put the Junior Circuit on top for good, 7-6. At the time, Gagne was in the midst of a record-setting streak of 84 straight regular-season saves. But the reaction in the AL dugout wasn't about beating the unbeatable. Many of the players believed that, come October, they could benefit from Blalock's blast.

"When Hank hit that home run," said then-A's pitcher Tim Hudson, "it was almost like he was a teammate with us in Oakland. He might have done something great for us."

In the end, it was the Yankees who benefited — somewhat. While they opened the Fall Classic at home, it didn't matter in the end. Florida won the Series in six, taking the decisive game in the Bronx.

MAKE IT COUNT Hank Blalock hit the AL's game-winning homer in the 2003 Midsummer Classic.

ALL-STAR GEAR

WHILE MONTHS OF BEHIND-THE-SCENES WORK IS PUT INTO preparing the host city and stadium for the All-Star Game, there is also a lot of attention and focus placed on the special gear made just for the Midsummer Classic.

For players, part of the fun of being selected to the All-Star team is getting their hands on limited edition swag. Among the spoils that go to every All-Star are four batting practice and four game jerseys — regular-season game jerseys with an All-Star patch. Majestic begins working on the designs for the next year's jerseys immediately after the previous All-Star Game. In one of the many charitable endeavors that mark the event, each player signs a BP and a game jersey, both of which are donated to the Baseball Assistance Team (B.A.T.), an MLB-run charity which helps all members of the extended baseball family.

"We work hand in hand with MLB Properties," said Chuck Strom, the director of MLB apparel at Majestic. "We'll review how the previous year's jerseys were received and performed. We'll put up the jerseys from the last 10 years, we'll have our design team in there and have a concept meeting. We definitely look to tie in the local market and history that should be incorporated into the design."

Majestic begins months in advance by producing jerseys for players who appear to be locks to win the fan vote or be selected to the two All-Star rosters. Some of the handiwork may ultimately go to waste, but with so much work to accomplish, it is imperative to get a head start. Of course, with roster alterations made right up until game day, there are nameplates and numbers being sewn onto jerseys in the hectic clubhouses just before the first pitch.

MLB and Majestic constantly look for ways to improve the jerseys, examining different fabrics and construction methods from one year to another. "We're always looking for the best products," said Steve Armus, vice president, domestic licensing, for MLB. "We want to deliver what the players want to wear."

Players sport their regular-season jerseys and caps, distinguishable by an All-Star patch. The weather is warm in most host cities in July, limiting the outerwear needed. While sweatshirts and caps with earflaps have become de rigueur in October, most players leaning on the dugout rail during the All-Star Game won't need extra garments. Nevertheless, partnerships are important in determining what new products are unveiled during the Midsummer Classic.

Fans annually clamor for batting practice jerseys, game jerseys and T-shirts featuring a player's name and number along with the All-Star logo. Fans love this Midsummer Classic gear so much that many have it before the players.

"As quickly as we can manufacture a player's jersey, we try to get it everywhere," said Strom. "You'll see David Wright jerseys at Citi Field once he's named, even before All-Star Week. Our goal is to get as many jerseys and products out as soon as possible."

In recent years, MLB has been working with Touch by Alyssa Milano and Victoria's Secret PINK, and All-Star materials have been particularly popular. These partnerships help MLB sell products that appeal to women. "Women shop differently than men," said Armus. "It's our job to pick great partners who are leaders in their businesses and who we can rely on and lean on."

As part of their relationships with MLB, licensees can imprint their All-Star gear with the official logo of the event. Those who are permitted to use the logo work closely with Ryan Samuelson, director, authentic collection, for MLB licensing, and often attempt to introduce new products or highlight popular gear. For example, Under Armour, MLB's official footwear supplier, produces the only cleats worn during the Midsummer Classic emblazoned with the All-Star logo. Similarly, Franklin and Rawlings produce the only batting gloves and helmets, respectively, featuring that logo. At the 2010 game, all participating players using Wilson gloves were able to wear the top-of-the-line A2000 in a red model honoring the host Anaheim Angels, which featured the All-Star logo and contest date.

To complete their uniforms, each player receives a dozen New Era hats that feature the All-Star logo. If a superstitious All-Star insists on wearing his sweat-stained lucky cap in the game, then an All-Star patch will be affixed to the cap with an on-site heat sealer. Similarly, a player can have an All-Star sticker applied to his regular-season batting helmet if he prefers to wear it during the game.

FASHION VICTIM

In the 1930s, the rivalry between the American and National leagues was more fierce than today's fans can perhaps understand. The leagues had separate administrations and separate sets of umpires, and players were almost never traded between them. The enmity between both circuits was palpable. So when the inaugural All-Star Game was played at the AL's Comiskey Park in Chicago in 1933, the National League, looking for a way to counter the Junior Circuit's superior lineup, decided that at least they could look sharp on the diamond. They took the field wearing road-gray flannels with "National League" stitched across the chest and caps with an "NL" insignia. The American League, which had its players wear the uniforms of their individual teams, defeated the Senior Circuit, 4-2. The NL jettisoned the matching uniform concept after just one year, and the 1933 contest remains the only All-Star Game in which all players on a team have worn the same uniform.

ALL ABOUT THE BALL

REGULAR SEASON, POSTSEASON OR ALL-STAR GAME, THE SPORT IS ALL ABOUT THE BALL. And for All-Star Week, there are actually four different baseballs that Rawlings produces. There's a ball for the XM All-Star Futures Game, two for the State Farm Home Run Derby — one regular, one gold ball, the latter a combination of a regular section of cowhide and a gold section — and the star of the show, the All-Star Game baseball. Each of the spheres contains a version of the All-Star logo, and the ball used for Tuesday's Midsummer Classic also features two-color stitching. "The ball is the centerpiece of the game, which makes the special one designed each year for the All-Star Game a great keepsake," said Ryan Samuelson, director, authentic collection, for MLB's licensing department.

The ball's design is determined about six months before the game every year, with special attention paid to the logo and colored stitching to make sure they won't affect hitters in any way. For example, MLB chooses an All-Star Game logo that doesn't use too much ink, recognizing that a more complex, filled-in design might make a ball's spin easier for a hitter to pick up during an at-bat. Once the design is set, the balls are produced at Rawlings' factory in Costa Rica, where, like all official balls, the 108 double-stitched seams are hand sewn.

The official balls used during All-Star Week events are the exact same product that can be found on shelves in sporting goods stores. In fact, when a ball is being produced, no one involved knows yet whether it will be going to the stadium for use in the game or to a store in some other far-off city.

BALL GAME Specially designed Midsummer Classic baseballs bear the All-Star Game logo.

TEDDY BALLGAME

TED WILLIAMS PLAYED IN JUST ONE WORLD SERIES DURING HIS 19-YEAR CAREER, AND HE batted a paltry .200 with just one RBI in the '46 Classic as his Red Sox fell to the Cardinals. Instead of making a name for himself in the Fall Classic as Babe Ruth and Joe DiMaggio had, Williams crafted some of his most momentous moments on the national stage in the All-Star Game.

Teddy Ballgame's first classic midsummer moment came in 1941 at Detroit's Briggs Stadium. When Williams came to bat with two outs in the bottom of the ninth, the game should have been over already. With one out, DiMaggio — owner of a then-48-game regular-season hitting streak — had grounded into what seemed like a game-ending double play. But he hustled down the line and beat out the throw by an eyelash, knocking in a run in the process, to keep the Junior Circuit alive with two outs and runners on the corners. Trailing, 5-4, the American League would have one more shot to win — and its best hitter at the plate.

"Ted had a great swing at a pitch and fouled it straight back," Red Sox teammate Dom DiMaggio — and brother of the Yankees' star — later recalled. "It's funny, but I thought to myself, if he had hit that fair, it would have gone over the roof. Then he hit the ball off the roof." Claude Passeau, the NL pitcher who had whiffed Williams just an inning earlier, "came in with that sliding fastball around my belt and I swung," Williams wrote in his autobiography, *My Turn at Bat*. "No cut-down protection swing, an all-out home run swing, probably with my eyes shut."

The ball flew far over the right-field wall for the first walk-off homer in All-Star history, and Williams — who at age 23 already had a reputation as a grouch — celebrated like an exuberant schoolkid, clapping his hands and jumping for joy. "It wasn't a fly ball, it was a line drive that just went straight up and hit the roof on a line," Dom said. "In all my years playing in that park, I never saw another one hit like that."

Williams was carried off the field by DiMaggio, who scored along with Joe Gordon on the home run, and AL starting pitcher Bob Feller, who, having already showered after leaving the game before the fourth inning, raced onto the field in his street clothes to celebrate the come-from-behind 7-5 win. With the longball, Williams finished the day 2 for 4, adding a double and knocking in four of the American League's eventual seven runs. Seven decades later, the homer remains among the most dramatic in All-Star annals and was the signature moment in the career of one of the best hitters who ever lived. "I've never been so happy," Williams wrote. "It was a wonderful, wonderful day."

Williams was drafted into military service after the 1942 season, but in '46 he returned to bat .342 with 123 RBI — and deliver another memorable All-Star Game home run. Williams' victim this time around was Pirates pitcher Rip Sewell, whose legs and feet had been shot to shreds five years earlier when a hunter mistook him for a deer. Forced to overhaul his delivery as a result, the right-hander devised the eephus, the most famous trick pitch in baseball history. Blooping high in the air like a slow-pitch softball offering, the eephus enabled Sewell to win 70 games with a 3.24 ERA from 1942–45.

"How he controlled it is anybody's guess," Williams later wrote. "It had a 20-foot-high arc. I remember watching him warm up, standing in the dugout with Bill Dickey, and saying to Dickey, 'Gee, I don't think you could ever generate enough power to hit that pitch out of the ballpark.' Nobody ever had."

Dickey advised Williams that the best approach might be a moving start, and in the 1946 Midsummer Classic, Williams tried exactly that, approaching the pitch as a softball hitter would. After building momentum with a few quick steps toward the mound, Williams timed the eephus and swung with all his might. "He hit it right out of there," Sewell said. "And I mean he *hit* it." The clout gave the AL a commanding 12-0 lead, and Williams remains the only Big League batter ever to hit the eephus for a homer.

SPLENDID SPLINTER
Ted Williams hit the first of two iconic Midsummer Classic homers in 1941.

CHAPTER 3: SUNDAY

WHILE TEAMS AROUND THE MAJORS ARE WRAPPING UP THE FIRST HALF of the season on the Sunday before the Midsummer Classic, the festivities have already begun in the host city of the All-Star Game. Whether or not they were lucky enough to score tickets to the main event, baseball fans of all ages flock to the annual FanFest held at a local convention center, which begins the Friday before the game and continues through Tuesday. Meanwhile, the All-Stars themselves begin descending on the host city on Sunday evening, often by way of private jet, as the host club's equipment managers provide a warm welcome. At the ballpark itself, the action commences with the Futures Game, featuring the top 50 prospects in the Minor Leagues. Once the stars of tomorrow have left the field, the spotlight is turned to baseball legends as they engage luminaries of stage and screen in a lighthearted softball game. Of course, it's not only famous faces that take the field during All-Star Week, as charitable events allow fans from all walks of life to participate.

MEDAL OF HONOR With so many events on Sunday, Minor League stars, MLB legends and charity 5K participants share the podium.

FUTURES GAME

I<small>N THE</small> *B<small>ACK TO THE</small> F<small>UTURE</small>* <small>FILM TRILOGY, TIME-TRAVELING SCIENTIST</small> Emmett "Doc" Brown offers two reasons for visiting the future: "Seeing the progress of mankind. I'll also be able to see who wins the next 25 World Series." While Major League Baseball's annual XM All-Star Futures Game, showcasing top Minor League talent, may not be able to grant such pre-science, it does provide something that sports fans dream of — a rare glimpse of what's in store for the game.

True to its mission, the Futures Game, the main event of Taco Bell All-Star Sunday, has been introducing fans to the next crop of young stars since its inaugural showcase in 1999. "It's always fun playing in a Big League stadium, playing in front of a lot of people," said Jeremy Hellickson, a Rays prospect who participated in Anaheim in 2010. "Just to play in a Futures Game, just to know that people think highly of you and want you to play in one the biggest games there is for Minor League players, it makes you feel good about yourself and all that you've accomplished so far."

More than 80 percent of participants eventually reach the Bigs, and the games have produced dozens of All-Stars; hurlers who have tossed no-hitters; home run champs; several Rookies of the Year; multiple Gold Glovers; more than a dozen Silver Sluggers; batting champs and MVPs in both leagues; and even a World Series MVP.

Hanley Ramirez owns one of those success stories. A top prospect with the Red Sox in 2005, he took part in the Futures Game when All-Star fever swung through Detroit. A perennial All-Star with the Marlins, Ramirez had quite an audience in his first national showcase.

"I remember watching him play in the All-Star Futures Game," said Red Sox slugger David Ortiz. "I saw him making a hell of a play against the wall, and after the game we were talking and I was like, 'Man, you're ready to be here.' It's a game that a lot of people should pay attention to because those kids coming up — that's the real future."

A total of 50 prospects take part each year — 25 composing a U.S. team and another 25 representing the World, the latter of whom wear jerseys bearing the flags of their native countries. Representatives from MLB, the MLB Scouting Bureau, MLB.com, *Baseball America*, USA Baseball and the 30 Big League clubs select the rosters for each squad, making sure to include one player from every organization. According to Mike Teevan, MLB's PR manager, young stars representing the host team are especially heralded, as was the case for Angels prospect and California native Hank Conger, the MVP of the 2010 Futures Game at Angel Stadium.

"For people in the Minor Leagues, obviously the main goal is to play in the Major Leagues, but I think the next highest is to be invited to the Futures Game," Conger said. "And for me to play right in my backyard is awesome."

Arguably the top crop of players starred in the 2003 Futures Game, when fans at Chicago's U.S. Cellular Field glimpsed Joe Mauer, Ryan Howard and Zack Greinke, among others, for the first time. That year,

FAST LANE Like many top prospects, Clay Buchholz arrived in the Majors not long after his Futures Game appearance.

44 players made their Futures Game debuts. And 43 of them went on to the Major Leagues.

Among the other success stories to emerge from the Futures Game is second baseman Chase Utley, an All-Star regular and World Series champ with the Phillies, who first showed his skills in 2001. The 15th overall selection in the 2000 First-Year Player Draft, Utley went 2 for 3 with a homer in the contest at the Mariners' Safeco Field. "This place is unbelievable and it gives you more than enough motivation to want to play in a ballpark like this every night," Utley said.

Held in the very ballpark that will host the Major League All-Star Game just two nights later, the Futures Game often provides players their first taste of life in The Show. Taking the field on Sunday nurtures the hope that they will someday be a part of the main event on Tuesday. And whether it's adjusting to picking up the ball amidst the backdrop of a three-tiered ballpark or mingling with top competition, the event can be an exhilarating experience.

"It was probably the biggest venue that I pitched in — the first Big League park where I pitched in front of 40,000 fans," Clay Buchholz said of his Futures Game performance at San Francisco's AT&T Park in 2007. "It was exciting for everybody."

All-Star Week provides the ideal platform for the Futures Game. As Teevan says, the contest "is like graduation for a lot of these guys. It's the last step." Giving young players a glimpse of the Majors, the contest allows them to showcase their skills on a national stage but also in a relaxed atmosphere, without the pressure of the game's final score or individual stat line.

MINOR LEAGUE ALL-STAR GAMES

Fifty of the top Minor League players are named to the two squads that participate in the annual MLB XM All-Star Futures Game as part of the All-Star festivities. But there is enough talent in the more than 200 teams — spread over more than a half-dozen leagues across various classes — to fill rosters in a bevy of Minor League All-Star contests.

A highlight of the Minor League All-Star circuit is the Triple-A clash between the Pacific Coast League and the International League. Similarly, the California and Carolina leagues match their top prospects at the Class-A level. The Southern League, Texas League, Florida State League, Midwest League and South Atlantic League all follow the Big League formula by matching the top players from one half of the circuit against the cream of the crop from the other. In a unique twist, the short-season New York–Penn League All-Star Game pits prospects from AL affiliates against those from NL farm clubs. Regardless of the format or the class designation, there is no shortage of classic contests in July.

"It's the Futures Game," said Wilkin Ramirez, a Tigers prospect selected to the 2010 World squad. "Personally, I don't like to lose, no matter where I play. But whether you win or lose, it's like you're winning anyway. You're already here."

ON DECK
Hank Conger, an Angels prospect and California resident, shined in 2010.

FIRST LOOK

ALTHOUGH THE FLYING CARS AND ROBOT MAIDS FROM *THE Jetsons* episodes were still not for sale and the Oceania of George Orwell's *1984* was not demarcated on any maps hung on schoolroom walls, there was no doubt that the future was upon baseball in the summer of 1999. With the 21st century just a few calendar pages away, Major League Baseball introduced the All-Star Futures Game — an annual event showcasing the sport's top prospects during the All-Star break.

"Major League Baseball is thrilled to give fans the unique opportunity of seeing some of our brightest young stars from around the world compete on the same field," said Jimmie Lee Solomon, executive vice president, baseball development, for Major League Baseball. "This game showcases the exceptional abilities of these players, who represent the future of Major League Baseball, on a national stage."

Played at Fenway Park in Boston, the inaugural Futures Game introduced fans to a young Yankees farmhand from the Dominican Republic named Alfonso Soriano. The wiry shortstop for the Double-A Norwich Navigators belted two homers and drove in five as he led the World squad to a 7-0 win.

"I can't imagine having a better afternoon," Soriano said after his performance in the game.

Having broken into the Majors at the end of the '99 campaign, Soriano would soon become a bona fide Big League star. In 2004, he would be the leading vote-getter for the All-Star Game and take home MVP honors from that year's Midsummer Classic.

NOW BOARDING

OF ALL THE FACETS OF ALL-STAR WEEK, ONE NECESSITY sometimes flies below the radar. But it's one of a few things without which the event literally can't happen. Getting the All-Stars into town is a process that has evolved considerably since the first Midsummer Classic in 1933, when the ballplayers arrived in Chicago via train. Today, even before the squad is named, traveling secretaries around the Majors start to arrange transportation for some players who are locks to make the team. For everyone else, the flights are booked the minute the rosters are announced.

The Midsummer Classic is supposed to be a reward for the All-Stars, so some teams charter private flights for their representatives, sometimes providing seats for family members, as well. And since the players fly to the host city on Sunday after their games, they will often share a plane with both their own teammates and the All-Stars from their opponent. In 2010, the Yankees finished the first half in Seattle, so Ichiro joined the Bombers' collection of All-Stars — a large contingent which included coaches, since New York had won the 2009 World Series — on the flight to Anaheim.

"We had a traveling party of between 40 and 50," said Ben Tuliebitz, the Yankees' traveling secretary. "We chartered a jet. We just figured it would be much more cost effective than having these guys fly private or trying to get everybody a first-class ticket from Seattle to Anaheim. And we knew that way we could have the plane leave as soon as the game was over, when we were ready for it."

Evan Longoria had a strange swing of emotions en route to the 2008 contest, with the Rays struggling for the first time all year. "It was a little bittersweet," Longoria said. "It was great to know I had made my first All-Star Game, but I was like, 'Man, we really need to pick this up as a team.' So we were sitting at the airport in Cleveland — it was myself and Scott Kazmir — and we were with Grady Sizemore and one of the coaches who was going to throw him batting practice for the Home Run Derby. It was just an interesting experience flying to Yankee Stadium, in its last year, for my first All-Star Game."

Players know that traveling to the host city in style is just the start of what will be a weekend full of highlights. "It's pretty sick," the Tigers' Justin Verlander said. "You go on a private jet and that's a little bit different. But once you get here and you start getting into the festivities and see all the people, then you start really getting excited about it."

> The Midsummer Classic is supposed to be a reward for the All-Stars, so some teams charter private flights for their representatives, sometimes providing seats for family members, as well.

CLUBHOUSE PASS

Just as they do during the regular season, the host team's equipment managers run the show in the clubhouses during All-Star Week. Visiting players are taken care of from the moment they arrive in town, being treated as if they are at home with their jerseys hanging from lockers marked by special All-Star Week nameplates.

For the equipment managers of the home team, the event is a grueling task, and it seems like the jobs never stop, whether it's setting locker assignments, handling all of the player equipment coming in from around the country or getting names and numbers sewn onto jerseys for players who are late additions to the team. With so many responsibilities and so many more players to account for than there are for a regular-season game, the equipment managers have their hands full throughout the long weekend.

"From '88 to today it's a whole different game," said Pirates Clubhouse Manager Scott Bonnett, who ran the home clubhouse during the 2006 All-Star Game at PNC Park as well as the 1988 affair when he was with the Reds. "The Home Run Derby used to be during the day and it wasn't as big as it is today, and you didn't have the Futures Game. It's a big production now. It gets bigger and better every year. They build on what they had and what's good."

Players from the home team keep their own lockers. When setting up the clubhouse, the equipment managers build out from there, arranging pitchers together, grouping players from the same team where possible, and working to organize the room in a way that will accommodate everyone.

In anticipation of the event, equipment managers often attend the previous year's All-Star Game, helping the host team while learning the ropes. "There is a lot to do during All-Star Week," said Ryan Samuelson, MLB's director, authentic collection. "We really rely on the equipment managers to help everything go smoothly."

The clubbies' most visible job is handling all of the various uniforms for the event. Walk into their corner of the clubhouse any time during All-Star Week, and you will see laundry racks filled with jerseys from the XM All-Star Futures Game and the Taco Bell Legends & Celebrity Softball Game, the BP jerseys that the players wear during Gatorade All-Star Workout Day and the regular-season jerseys for the game itself. Majestic Athletic, MLB's official on-field uniform supplier, sends batches of blank jerseys, along with lettering kits and numbers, to the host ballpark. Heat presses are operating constantly to get patches and names onto jerseys in time for the events.

IMPROV

Tigers second baseman Lou Whitaker was one of the greatest players of his generation, but he was as distinguished for his absentmindedness as his glovework. This was never more apparent than at the 1985 All-Star Game, when Whitaker showed up to Minneapolis's Metrodome without any equipment — not even a uniform. "I left all my stuff in the trunk of my Mercedes back home," he told the *Chicago Tribune*. "Ain't that a shame?" Whitaker was able to borrow a glove from Cal Ripken Jr., but he had to cover the brand name with tape because the glove wasn't produced by the company with which he had an endorsement deal. Getting a uniform was more complicated. The Tigers sent a new one via express delivery, but it got lost in transit. Forced to improvise, Whitaker sent a clubbie to a local sporting goods store to buy a Tigers replica jersey. Using a black marker, he scrawled his uniform No. 1 on the back. After the mad pregame scramble, the All-Star Game itself was anticlimactic — Whitaker played five innings and flied out twice.

IDENTITY CRISIS

On July 4, 1998, the Dodgers bolstered their club for the stretch run by shipping prospects Paul Konerko and Dennys Reyes to Cincinnati in exchange for All-Star closer Jeff Shaw. Since there was just one game left before the All-Star break, the Dodgers decided to have Shaw fly directly to Coors Field for the Midsummer Classic. The team shipped his new jersey to Denver overnight, and Shaw became the only player to represent a club in the All-Star Game without ever having played for that team. The Dodgers forgot to send the rest of the uniform, though, so Shaw had to borrow Raul Mondesi's pants and Gary Sheffield's shoes. Asked if he felt like a Dodger yet, Shaw quipped, "I feel like a Dodger outfielder."

SHOWTIME

As if the elite ballplayers in town for All-Star Week aren't enough of a star-studded cast, Major League Baseball brings out the game's former greats and well-known entertainers for a game of softball that is always a crowd-pleaser. Since 2001 in Seattle, the All-Star Legends & Celebrity Softball Game has followed the All-Star Futures Game on Sunday's schedule.

"It just keeps getting better because you see guys like Freddie Lynn and Goose Gossage," said James Denton, star of the hit ABC show *Desperate Housewives*. "These guys are so nice, especially Ozzie Smith, that you kind of become friends with them. It's an annual thing, and as a baseball fan, that's really exciting."

MLB erects a temporary outfield wall on the host field to create a much smaller area extending 225 feet down the lines and just 237 feet to straightaway center. The five-inning game matches the AL and NL, with the celebs choosing which Big League team, and thus which league, they represent. ESPN records the game and airs it after Monday night's Home Run Derby. "It's fun to see different people from different walks of entertainment and to be a part of the entertainment for the great baseball fans that come here," said Gossage.

Although score is kept, most of the attention is paid to the antics on the field between players, who are miked for the ESPN broadcast and for fans in the stadium. "I mean, this is Disneyland," said Food Network personality Guy Fieri, who participated in 2010 when the game came to Anaheim. "This is Disney Baseball Land."

For many of the celebs with busy schedules in front of the cameras, there's another priority in addition to the fun. "My entire thing about any of these is try not to get hurt, try not to hurt anybody else and try not to embarrass myself," said Jon Hamm, who stars as Don Draper on TV's *Mad Men*. "If I can manage that, I think I'll be alright."

Some of the celebrities, who often spend their days dodging fans and paparazzi cameras, can get plenty fanboy-ish themselves when surrounded by the game's all-time greats.

"I got lucky today," Denton said of the 2010 game. "I accidentally went over to the wrong hotel because I didn't know where the bus was. And they said, 'It's over there,' and I ended up on the legends' bus. So, I was the only actor on the bus with all the players. I know they thought I did it on purpose, but it was a completely honest accident — but a good one. It was definitely the 'cool kids' bus.'"

CAST PARTY Actor Jon Hamm met (from left) former ballplayers Ozzie Smith, Jennie Finch, Gary Carter and Mike Piazza in 2010.

LAUGH IN
Hall of Fame hurler
Goose Gossage and
late-night talk show
host Jimmy Kimmel
share a joke during
2004 All-Star Week.

STAR POWER Model Marisa Miller and Mike Piazza soak in the Legends & Celebrity Softball Game in 2010.

RACE DAY

F<small>ANS IN TOWN FOR THE</small> M<small>IDSUMMER</small> C<small>LASSIC FESTIVITIES CAN</small> partake in myriad charitable events. In 2009 and 2010, fans could lace up their sneakers on the Sunday morning before the All-Star Game to compete in the All-Star Game Charity 5K and Fun Run. Not only did participants get a chance to meet baseball legends, but they also helped to raise money for cancer research.

With so many ways to indulge their passion for baseball during All-Star Week, it can be hard for fans to find time to help those in need while visiting the host city, which made the Charity 5K and Fun Run presented by Sports Authority and Nike a great part of the calendar. The race, which was inaugurated in St. Louis during All-Star Week in 2009 and repeated in 2010 in Anaheim, benefitted several cancer charities, including Stand Up 2 Cancer, Susan G. Komen for the Cure, the Prostate Cancer Foundation and, in 2010, local Southern California–based charity City of Hope.

"We're so grateful for the support Major League Baseball has given Komen," said Katrina McGhee, senior vice president of global business development and partnerships, Susan G. Komen for the Cure. "Breast cancer is not only difficult for the patient — it's a diagnosis that affects the entire family. The awareness created by Major League Baseball's support of Komen enables us to help families around the world in our promise to end breast cancer forever."

The 2010 race in Anaheim attracted 9,209 participants, up from about 8,000 in 2009. But of much greater significance was the money raised — more than $300,000 for the four charities, which more than doubled the St. Louis total. MLB donated 100 percent of the registration fees, and additional sponsorships helped boost Anaheim's total, as well. MLB also enlisted the help of its many business partners in staging the event.

"We are delighted to be part of the All-Star Game Charity 5K and Fun Run presented by Nike and are grateful to Major League Baseball for its support of our efforts to help patients everywhere conquer cancer," said Michael A. Friedman, M.D., City of Hope president and chief executive officer and director of City of Hope Comprehensive Cancer Center in 2010. "We are pleased to be alongside the Prostate Cancer Foundation, Stand Up 2 Cancer and Susan G. Komen for the Cure, as we all work as partners in these lifesaving efforts."

The races began early in the morning, with many participants arriving before they got underway to stake out the booths set up near the start line, which featured everything from Nike retail offerings to a wall on which runners could sign their names and voice their support for Stand Up 2 Cancer's cause.

MLB hired a local run-management company, which worked with USA Track & Field, to map out the course, ensuring that the distances were correct and that everything was in order. The 2010 course started in the Angel Stadium parking lot and wound its way along the surrounding streets before ending with a lap around the stadium's warning track. The whole process, from setting the track to getting permits to finding sponsors and promoting the race took about a year of planning.

BORN TO RUN
The 2010 All-Star Charity 5K and Fun Run gave participants a real treat — the route led them around the Angel Stadium warning track.

Assisting at the 2010 start line were a number of officials from Major League Baseball and representatives from the various charities involved in the event, as well as former players like Hall of Famers Rod Carew and Paul Molitor, and Angels fan-favorites Tim Salmon and Bobby Grich. Hall of Fame outfielder and perennial All-Star Reggie Jackson, who spent five seasons with the California Angels, also made a surprise visit on behalf of the Prostate Cancer Foundation to show his support for the cause. Joining them were celebrities like Jillian Michaels, from NBC's *The Biggest Loser,* and award-winning actress Gabrielle Union.

"In your mind you're just showing up thinking, 'I'm going to hand out a few medals,'" Salmon said. "And then almost 10,000 people show up and you're like, 'Oh my gosh, is this what the New York Marathon looks like?' We got kind of a feel for somebody that's never been around that environment, but as far as people coming out for the cause, I mean, all the cancer awareness that people came out to support is monumental.

"None of us are immune from it — if we don't have it, someone in our family has it or someone that we know has it. So just to see people come out and support such a great cause is awesome."

Vivien Wadeck from North Hollywood, Calif., won the first two 5Ks for the women, posting a time of 17:49 in Anaheim. For the men, Conor Stanton, an 18-year-old from Fullerton, Calif., had a winning time of 15:47 in 2010. But it was hard to find anyone in the crowd — from the runners to the many families that participated in the accompanying one-mile walk — who didn't feel like a part of something huge.

"I was touched most by the showings of families that participated in the mile family walk/run," Molitor said. "They're doing things together and coming out for the cause. Kids learn at young ages the importance of giving back and serving. I came away kind of encouraged by the old human spirit coming through again. It was a great morning."

PITCH, HIT AND RUN

Ever wonder how those lucky kids end up in the outfield during the Home Run Derby? Many of those children are finalists in the Aquafina Pitch, Hit and Run (PHR) program, a national contest that judges kids ranging in age from 7 to 14 on their ability to pitch, hit and, you guessed it, run. When the competition began it only included baseball, but a softball component was added in 2010.

The competition begins on a local level, with kids taking part in one of the more than 4,000 events — that includes more than 600,000 hopefuls — across the country, with the top finishers advancing. Eventually, the winners take their talents to Major League parks around the country for a semi-final round.

Finally, the champions of each division (7–8, 9–10, 11–12 and 13–14) are decided on All-Star Monday before the State Farm Home Run Derby, and the overall champ is honored in a ceremony during the Derby. In 2010, U.S. Olympic gold medal softball players Jennie Finch and Natasha Watley were on hand for the celebration.

To judge pitching, PHR has its competitors throw at a strike zone. Each time the pitcher hits the strike zone, he or she earns points. For hitting, the competitors hit off a tee and are scored based on how far the ball carries. Finally, the kids are timed running the bases.

HELPING HANDS

WITH SPORTS FANS AROUND THE WORLD FIXATED ON THE ALL-Star events, MLB uses the exposure to bring attention to some worthy causes and make a difference for those in need. Through a variety of programs, MLB helps raise money for numerous local charities and provides hundreds of kids with once-in-a-lifetime opportunities.

"Each year we incorporate activities into All-Star that extend beyond the field and make a difference in the community," said Tim Brosnan, MLB's executive vice president, business. "When All-Star Week comes to a conclusion, there should be a community legacy left in the host city."

On the Friday before the All-Star Game, the Jr. RBI Classic opens the festivities. RBI (Reviving Baseball in Inner Cities) is a charitable initiative that brings baseball and softball to kids in underserved communities. Friday's events begin with a tournament that consists of more than 40 friendly games between baseball and softball teams comprised of 11- and 12-year-olds from cities throughout the country. Later, experts work with the teams to teach a wide range of drills, covering almost every facet of the game including hitting, pitching and baserunning. When All-Star FanFest begins, these teams participate in the event's legends clinics. The RBI teams also receive uniforms, equipment and All-Star Game apparel to get them ready to attend the XM All-Star Futures Game, Taco Bell All-Star Legends & Celebrities Softball Game and the State Farm Home Run Derby. Overall, the Jr. RBI Classic provides an unforgettable baseball experience for young kids who are sure to be fans for life.

"The annual Jr. RBI Classic is a great way to include these young boys and girls in MLB All-Star Week," said RBI Program Director David James. "The first two Jr. RBI Classic events in St. Louis and Anaheim were such successes, and we are looking forward to providing these kids with more once-in-a-lifetime experiences in the future."

During the Home Run Derby, MLB continues to provide opportunities for kids. Every time a contestant blasts a ball deep, State Farm donates $3,000 to local Boys & Girls Clubs. However, when a hitter has nine outs, the stakes are raised and a gold ball comes into play.

Each time the gold ball is hit out of the yard, State Farm increases its donation to $17,000 for the youth centers. In 2010, this led to a total of $573,000 raised for Boys & Girls Clubs in Anaheim.

In addition to donating funds to improve the lives of kids away from the field, MLB provides an opportunity for disabled children to live out their on-field dreams in the Challenger-Champions Game. In the contest, which features local teams from the Little League Challenger and PONY Champions divisions, disabled children play a one-inning game against Big League mascots. The event provides an unforgettable chance for these children to succeed on a Major League field and receive encouragement from those in attendance.

Each year, the Make-a-Wish Foundation also partners with MLB to make dreams into realities for kids with terminal conditions. The children are greeted by Futures Game players and Major League mascots upon arrival, and they spend time with the same players before dinner. They're also given personalized All-Star jerseys and gift bags before being taken on a full tour of the ballpark, from the clubhouse to the press box. The fun just starts there, as the kids then have the chance to explore FanFest, attend a meet-and-greet session with baseball legends and current All-Stars, and relax in a private viewing suite for the Futures Game, the Legends & Celebrity Softball Game, the Home Run Derby and the All-Star Game.

While all eyes rest on the host city, baseball makes the attention worth its while, providing significant charitable contributions. In '07, MLB teamed with Fox Sports Net (FSN) Bay Area for the Stay in School Challenge, a program that addresses attendance in middle and high schools. Included in the program were five All-Star teachers in the Bay Area, one of whom, Michael Meneses, was named the 2007 Bay Area All-Star Teacher. Meneses received $10,000 for his school and was recognized by the San Francisco Giants. MLB and the Giants also donated almost $4 million of the net proceeds from Gatorade All-Star Workout Day to local and national charities. Finally, after the All-Star Gala and Pregame Party, MLB donates perishable food items to local food banks throughout the community.

FIELDS OF GREEN

With so many events during All-Star Week, MLB makes every effort to put on as "green" a show as possible.

"Major League Baseball recognizes its civic responsibility to conduct environmentally friendly practices," said John McHale Jr., executive vice president, administration, and chief information officer for MLB. "Thanks to the guidance of the Natural Resources Defense Council (NRDC) and the support of the host club, MLB's commitment to going green is on display throughout All-Star Week."

Working with the NRDC, MLB's efforts extended across the 2010 Midsummer Classic, from renewable energy credits to offset the power used in the stadium to a red carpet made of 100 percent recycled fiber content for the parade of All-Stars to "Green Teams" roving the stadium and collecting recyclables from fans. The initiative extended beyond the ballpark, too, with consideration being given to sustainable materials used for the paper for programs, invitations and tickets to bio-based products, such as cups and cutlery, at events such as the All-Star Gala.

KIDS' SUMMER CLASSIC
Members of Jr. RBI teams head
to town to get All-Star treatment
during the week's events.

CHAPTER 4: COVERING THE ACTION

BASEBALL IS AMERICA'S PASTIME, AND ITS ENTHUSIASTS ARE NUMEROUS. BUT few of these fans will get the chance to experience the Midsummer Classic in person. Fortunately, that doesn't exclude them from a second of the action. Of course, All-Star coverage is not limited to our national boundaries. Turn on a radio, a television or a computer — virtually anywhere in the world — in mid-July, and there is bound to be All-Star Week baseball. From TBS's exclusive broadcast of the *Selection Show* announcing the rosters to MLB Network's never-before-seen press conference footage to the clamor for the *Official All-Star Game Program* on sale throughout the host city, baseball is in hot supply. And the media covering All-Star events can sometimes seem just as plentiful as the fans. With reporters filling not one but two press boxes at the stadium, photographers capturing intimate images of the players interacting and broadcasters providing up-to-the-minute analysis, excitement from baseball's Midsummer Classic is always flowing.

IN FOCUS Photographers flock to the action, as they did at Minute Maid Park in 2004, to capture All-Star memories.

SELECTION SHOW

THROUGHOUT HIS CAREER AS ONE OF BASEBALL'S PREMIER CLOSERS, DENNIS ECKERSLEY GOT very used to stepping into precarious situations at the last minute with little time to prepare. And it's a good thing he has that high-wire experience, because as a member of the on-air team hosting TBS's *All-Star Selection Show*, things haven't changed all that much.

The annual show, which launched in 2007, is the first official place fans can learn of the All-Star team selections. Even Eckersley and fellow hosts Cal Ripken Jr. and David Wells are in the dark about who they will be discussing until less than 24 hours before the live broadcast. They get the final rosters the night before the show, which airs on Sunday afternoon the week before the All-Star break. The analysts must be in the studio by 8 a.m. preparing to go live, which doesn't leave a lot of time to get ready for their hour-long on-air discussion of all the players who have been voted in by the fans — and even those who have been snubbed. "They don't tell us who's on the list till the last minute, so you've got to be on top of it. You have to be ready because there are so many players to talk about," said Eckersley. "We need to deal with a lot of information. Normally you have time to mess around [on-air] but with this show it's, 'Hey, how are you?' and bang! You're into it."

Realistically, there's no way that the 60-plus players picked for the All-Star Game will receive the same amount of discussion time on the air. That's why Eckersley, Ripken and Wells spend their pre-show time deciding which All-Stars they most want to talk about and divvying up who will discuss each one. "It all comes down to one or two positions that are up for grabs, so you're never really surprised [by the players selected]," said Eckersley. "You pick a few guys you want to talk about. For each position, we'll be like kids trading baseball cards: 'You get him. You can have this guy.'"

Since the bulk of the show features analysis from the on-air talent, there's not much time for interviews. Still, producers usually pre-record some with the managers for each league, along with a couple of freshly minted All-Stars, to roll in at the appropriate time. And whenever possible, Eckersley tries to highlight the guys on the roster who might not otherwise get much airtime.

"If you're from Pittsburgh, nobody talks about you except when you step forward on the field and take your hat off," said the Hall of Famer. "When I made my first All-Star Game, I was with the Indians and people didn't care much about them. That was the only time everybody knew who I was. So if I was still playing, I'd *love* to be on this selection show."

TBS's *Selection Show* also features a surprise for viewers — the 10 players who will compete for fans' online votes to win the final roster spot in each league are revealed. The Final Vote announcement adds yet another special element to a show that Eckersley considers pretty special already. "People start really paying attention to baseball at the All-Star Game," said Eckersley, "and this is the show that introduces the All-Star Game, so it's important."

NIGHTTIME CLASSIC

Previously a daytime affair, the 1967 All-Star Game was the first to air on prime-time television on the East Coast, and it attracted some 55 million viewers — nearly five times the number who had watched the year before. It was the largest TV audience ever for a non–World Series game, and millions of viewers went to sleep satisfied — albeit bleary-eyed — after a 15-inning classic.

An afternoon affair in Anaheim — the local start time was 4:15 p.m. — made the game difficult for hitters, whose vision was impaired by the sun's glare. The result was a record 30 combined strikeouts and a 1-1 tie after nine frames. The deadlock continued until the 15th, when 21-year-old Catfish Hunter, hurling his fifth inning of relief, gave up a game-winning homer to Cincinnati's Tony Perez. "I feel like a king," Perez said afterward, and nobody was arguing.

IN THE HOT SEAT
Dennis Eckersley's poise under pressure as a Major League closer now helps him on-air during TBS's *All-Star Selection Show.*

PRIME-TIME TALENT
Harold Reynolds (left) and Greg
Amsinger anchored MLB Network's
coverage of the 2010 festivities.

MLB NETWORK

IN ITS FRESHMAN CAMPAIGN IN 2009, MLB NETWORK proved that it had what it takes to stand with the big guys. With less than a full season of coverage under its belt, the Network joined the broadcast contingent for the '09 All-Star Game at Busch Stadium after a record-setting cable TV launch on Jan. 1. At the 2010 Midsummer Classic in Anaheim, the Network bolstered its programming to provide insatiable viewers with even more in-depth coverage.

"As all of the events during All-Star Week are created with fans in mind, it was important to increase MLB Network's number of live hours of coverage around [the 2010] All-Star Game," said MLB Network President and CEO Tony Petitti.

Such in-depth coverage requires tremendous resources, and MLB Network learned what to expect from its initial All-Star broadcast in '09. Airing the show on the road presents logistical challenges, as the setup of technical equipment must be coordinated. The Network's All-Star planning begins early in the year, with weekly meetings to determine the elements — such as feature broadcasts, interviews and live coverage — that will fill the many hours of All-Star Week programming. In addition to broadcasting the All-Stars during the media availability sessions on Monday, MLB Network airs *MLB Tonight* — its nightly regular-season show — live from batting practice during Gatorade All-Star Workout Day, which also takes place on Monday.

"Going into 2009, we had never done an All-Star Game, but we felt it could be another layer of coverage," John Entz, senior vice president of production for MLB Network, said of the Network's All-Star Monday batting practice coverage. "You want to take people where they don't get to go. With a field full of All-Stars, it makes for compelling TV."

On Tuesday, coverage shifts to the pregame *Red Carpet Show* — highlighted by the parade of All-Stars — before the players take the field. *MLB Tonight* goes live again after the game.

One aspect of All-Star Week that fans had never seen before 2009 was the formal press conference. MLB Network made sure that the Monday event, which typically precedes a more casual media session with the players, was televised, giving fans four hours of inside access. In addition to that inside coverage, 11 hours of live programming were shown directly from Anaheim, the highlight of which was the Network's 115 interviews — 57 of them with members of the 2010 All-Star teams, two featuring Hall of Famers and others with assorted members of each league's coaching staff.

> *"Going into 2009, we had never done an All-Star Game. You want to take people where they don't get to go. With a field full of All-Stars, it makes for compelling TV."* **—John Entz**

MLB Network brought 13 members of its on-air talent team to the 2010 game, including Bob Costas, Peter Gammons and a host of former All-Stars such as Harold Reynolds, Sean Casey and Al Leiter. But even with such an experienced broadcast team and a carefully scheduled slate of programming, the Network has experienced some unpredictable moments — most notably the passing of longtime New York Yankees Owner George Steinbrenner on July 13, 2010, the day of the All-Star Game. "You can prepare as much as you want," said Entz, "but you have to be flexible for what you can't control."

The crew responded to the news quickly, with veteran analysts Tom Verducci, Gammons and Leiter among those going on the air during MLB Network's special features about Steinbrenner before transitioning the show into its scheduled All-Star coverage. Some of that coverage included an interview with Commissioner Bud Selig conducted by Costas — a conversation about Steinbrenner's passing, Nationals rookie phenomenon Stephen Strasburg, the use of instant replay and daytime World Series games.

Although the Steinbrenner news brought a certain gravity to the 2010 broadcast, much of the programming during All-Star Week was lighter in nature. There was a guest appearance from comic actor Will Ferrell, who was at Angel Stadium for the Home Run Derby, and tape-delay coverage of the *Red Carpet Show*, which in Anaheim traveled down Disneyland's Main Street USA.

"The setting of Disneyland was just perfect. I don't think that we can get better," Entz said. MLB Network took a unique approach to its FanFest exhibit leading up to the 2010 Midsummer Classic, allowing attendees to record virtual interviews with on-air personalities Reynolds and Hazel Mae at its exhibit.

Additional programming in 2009 included three features from Costas: a look back at the 1999 Midsummer Classic at Boston's Fenway Park, a detailed history of baseball in St. Louis and an anniversary tribute to the 1964 All-Star Game at Shea Stadium. In similar fashion, footage from the 1965 Midsummer Classic, a 6-5 National League victory originally called by broadcasters Jack Buck and Joe Garagiola, re-aired for the first time ever during the 2010 festivities. "Once the game was in our hands, we felt that it was something people would want to see," said Entz, who called the contest a "true throwback."

"It was fascinating how TV worked back then, how it showed baseball compared to now."

PRESIDENTIAL ADDRESS
President Barack Obama (center) joined Fox announcers Joe Buck (right) and Tim McCarver in the broadcast booth in 2009.

ON AIR

WHEN THE ALL-STAR GAME STAKES WERE RAISED IN 2003 TO AWARD the winning league home-field advantage in that year's Fall Classic, things didn't just get more intense for the players. The ante was also upped for the Fox crew that broadcasts the game to fans.

Before Commissioner Bud Selig raised the stakes in the Midsummer Classic, the network would air all sorts of lighthearted, pre-recorded pieces about the players, their off-field lives and their performance that season. "But now," said Pete Macheska, Fox's lead producer for the telecast, "the game moves faster, and we don't want to squeeze all these things in. So we focus more on the game itself, where there's strategy to talk about."

Using a crew of approximately 50 people, Fox begins work on the next year's game almost as soon as the current one ends. The preparation that takes place in advance of the game involves everything from scouting camera locations around the host ballpark and prepping the announcer's booth to deciding what packages to pre-tape and air during the game. As game day gets closer, producers also reach out to the players to determine who is willing to wear a microphone on the field. And even though they have something significant to play for, the stars from both leagues are usually amenable to being wired for sound during the game.

"Everybody at home wonders, 'What do they talk about on first base? What does the catcher say to the pitcher when they're out there on the mound?'" said Macheska. "So in a game that counts but really doesn't, the players are more relaxed and we can find the answers to those questions. It's a way of personalizing them to the fans."

Fox producers are constantly trying to develop new ways to bridge the gap between the stars and those who follow them. Some new developments have already made their way into the broadcast, such as the Diamond Cam, a tiny camera anchored four inches beneath the ground between home plate and the pitcher's mound, and 2010's airing of the game in 3D. Other innovations, such as interviews with batters in the dugout just before their turn in the on-deck circle, have yet to see the light of day largely because there's just no time for them in the broadcast. Whether it's because players are swinging at more first pitches or managers are making more frequent personnel moves early in the game, the All-Star Game now moves too swiftly to include every technical trick Macheska would like to try.

That's not to say Fox doesn't allot time for unique elements, such as inviting President Barack Obama up to the broadcast booth during the 2009 game. "It all happened seamlessly. And we couldn't believe how much he knew about the game," said Macheska. "He made our announcers — Joe Buck and Tim McCarver — feel at ease, and that came across. It was just fun, and for us at Fox, any time we can get fun into the broadcast, we do."

At least until the game nears the final innings. Then, it's time for both the players and the broadcasting team to buckle down. "You used to have players who might not be in the dugout at the end of the game, but one thing you'll notice since the games started counting, all of the players are on the top step," Macheska said. "They're there to see who is going to win. This is an exhibition game that's not an exhibition game, and that's the challenge for us. They are taking the game more seriously, so we have to also."

HOMER HAPPY
ESPN sideline reporter Erin Andrews interviewed Justin Morneau after he won the 2008 Home Run Derby.

ESPN TV

IF YOU THINK OF THE ALL-STAR GAME AS A BASEBALL FEAST, THEN WATCHING THE HOME RUN Derby is kind of like getting to eat your dessert before the big meal. The event that takes place the night before the leagues battle it out features nothing but the treat that fans devour — the longball. And in the 18 years that ESPN has been airing the home run competition, it's become one of its most popular broadcasts of the summer. Over the last five years, the Derby has averaged nearly 7.5 million viewers, and the network also broadcasts a pre-recorded celebrity softball game the night before the All-Star Game that averages more than 3.5 million viewers. There's a very simple reason for its popularity.

"The event itself has a uniqueness to it because unlike in a baseball game, where the possibility of a home run is a question, here it's a certainty they will be hit — and hit in large numbers," said Jed Drake, senior vice president and executive producer for ESPN. "These are the best hitters in the game, and you're guaranteed to see something monumental in terms of baseball repeatedly."

The Derby contestants often make it look easy, launching bomb after bomb out of the stadium, but capturing those mammoth blasts for TV is anything but a walk in the ballpark. ESPN uses approximately 100 crew members for the Home Run Derby alone, along with 25 different cameras. And since ESPN started telecasting the event in 1993, Drake said that the network has had lengthy debates about shaking up its camera work to find new and different ways to watch balls as they fly out of the park every year. The conversations have resulted in such innovations as Ball Track, technology that instantly lets viewers know the height, distance and speed of the home runs, and Ultra Mo, which slows the ball down for the ultimate look at the best shots.

There is also debate about changing the angles from which cameras view home runs, but while "variety is good for the sake of variety," said Drake, "the question is whether it's best for the viewer." That's why ESPN still employs the high home plate shot and "the flash position" — cameras in right and left fields that pick up the ball off the bat. It may seem like the task of the camera operators is fairly simple — follow a ball as it flies out of the ballpark — yet tracking a small white target 350 feet or more away can be as much of a challenge for them as hitting a homer is for the players.

"The camera crew gets excited about showing off their skills and abilities, and they enjoy getting to follow [hits] that never exist the rest of the year when they're covering games," said Drake. "The uniqueness of the event allows them to do something not in the realm of their day to day."

As compelling as the home runs are, though, the heart of Derby coverage is in the reactions and interactions of the players on the field. It's a rare opportunity for ESPN to place mics and cameras where they couldn't during a regular-season game. All of that is done to get up close and personal. "What you want is a glimpse of the players acting as they would if they were in the clubhouse, in a way the public doesn't normally see them," said Drake. Because the next day, they'll be all business as each league tries to best the other in the All-Star Game.

"The Derby is one thing done purely for fun during those couple of days," said Drake. "That's why you see the enjoyment on the players' faces." And that's part of why the fans at home enjoy the event so much.

The Derby is a rare opportunity for ESPN to place mics and cameras where they couldn't during a regular-season game. "What you want is a glimpse of the players acting as they would if they were in the clubhouse, in a way the public doesn't normally see them." —Jed Drake

OVER THE AIRWAVES

IN RECENT YEARS, THE MIDSUMMER CLASSIC HAS EVOLVED into a made-for-TV spectacle, but that doesn't mean that the game has abandoned its radio roots. ESPN Radio's broadcast of the All-Star Game airs on approximately 350 stations, as well as on XM Satellite Radio. That's an audience of millions tuning in on 504 nationwide affiliates to hear a production that is constantly seeking new ways to *expand* listener access and interest. The game, which ESPN Radio has aired for the past 14 seasons, poses a unique challenge for producers, requiring the same level of coverage as a playoff game but without that win-or-go-home storyline.

"It's a fun atmosphere," said John Martin, senior director and executive producer of ESPN Radio's event productions. "So for us, it's about bringing the bigness of the event to the listener to convey the emotion and intensity that's going on in the park."

The process of pulling the production together is relatively simple. Martin and his crew of 15 travel a few months before the July contest to survey the host ballpark, and they are usually offered access to the home team's radio booth for their broadcast. But that booth is already hard-wired for the home team's equipment, which can be different from ESPN's. Rather than rip up the existing wiring for just one game, they often use the visiting booth instead. Other technical concerns arise, too, like making certain there's a clear channel to broadcast on. There have been occasions when another broadcaster has tried to send a signal on the same channel ESPN was using, which means that nothing but a garbled message is going out to fans, so keeping a clear frequency is a top priority from the get-go.

Once all of the technical details are sorted out, the biggest challenge is capturing the ambience of the evening and giving listeners an up-close-and-personal impression of their favorite players during the game. One of the broadcast's major innovations has been on-field, in-game interviews. "We put a reporter in each dugout," said Martin. "This is an exhibition, so you have the freedom to talk to guys as they're coming in and out of the game. We can throw down to our reporters, who will have A-Rod or Derek Jeter, and get two or three questions in. We focus on nuts and bolts stuff. So when they're talking to us, they're a little more relaxed and a little bit more forthcoming."

As part of the desire to bring listeners as close to the action as possible, the pre- and post-game radio shows both originate on the field. Such access comes at a cost, though, as the on-air talent — a group that has included the likes of Charlie Steiner, Dan Shulman, Kevin Kennedy and Dave Campbell over the years — has no computers on the field and is without easy access to statistics. The talent has to rely on producers in an outside studio to feed them information as quickly as possible.

Still, Martin likes being outside of "a sterile studio" for a production like the All-Star Game; it's another way of making listeners feel like they're a part of an event that's intended as a treat for devoted fans. "We don't have the benefit of pictures, so we paint the pictures in your mind," Martin said. "We want you to clearly hear the elation and emotion in the ballpark. But a little imagination is a wonderful thing."

MLB.COM

MLB.COM OFFERS A GLOBAL BASEBALL AUDIENCE THE CHANCE to participate in the festivities that comprise All-Star Week. Thanks to a wide array of comprehensive editorial content, high quality multimedia and commerce (tickets, memorabilia, apparel, etc.) any fan with Internet access can keep up with all the action.

The website offers unparalleled information about the All-Star teams, including interactive player rosters with video, bios and statistics. The site also contains extensive highlights and reference material from past All-Star Games, including year-by-year results and Most Valuable Players, all-time leaders, records, selections and managers, among other features. MLB.com provides the deepest, broadest, most timely and most substantive editorial coverage of all

the exciting events surrounding the main event. It's also the source for the most technologically advanced video and graphic real-time features available online, providing fans with a unique opportunity to interact with the Midsummer Classic — for example, by voting for the Ted Williams All-Star Game Most Valuable Player Award presented by Chevrolet. MLB.com provides live HD quality video streaming of All-Star Week events, including batting practice and press conferences.

In addition, MLB.com broadcasts live from All-Star FanFest with celebrity interviews, specialty programming and the Commissioner's annual town hall chat. The site delivers must-see daily galleries with behind-the-scenes photos from every All-Star Week event.

INTERNATIONAL

THERE'S NO DENYING THAT BASEBALL IS AS AMERICAN AS A SPORT CAN GET. BUT WHEN IT comes to broadcasting the All-Star Game, it has become a true international event. Whether it's being watched by a rabid fan base across Asia, Latin America and Canada, U.S. soldiers stationed abroad, expatriates in Europe or those just discovering the game in China, the Midsummer Classic now airs in 220 countries and territories around the world, in 20 different languages.

"The All-Star Game showcases the best players in baseball, many of whom are born outside of the United States," said Paul Archey, MLB's senior vice president, international business operations. "Fans around the globe have a tremendous passion for the game of baseball. Along with our broadcast partners, we are committed to promoting and growing the game internationally."

While Fox uses its own crew to broadcast the game to a predominately domestic audience, Major League Baseball International (MLBI) produces an ad-free worldwide feed of the All-Star showcase. MLBI utilizes its own team to customize the audio and video for rightsholders across the globe — 50 in 2010. The international production uses eight cameras and two 53-foot mobile units, featuring mini control rooms and a transmission area.

English-speaking networks typically air the commentary of MLBI announcers Gary Thorne and Rick Sutcliffe, but those broadcasting in other languages will have hosts who listen to the audio track and translate it at studios in their countries. In addition, foreign broadcasters come on-site each year and take advantage of the fully-equipped broadcast booths provided by MLB. In 2010, 10 rightsholders, including the Armed Forces Network, Fox Deportes (Latin America), ESPN Deportes (Latin America), Fuji TV and NHK (Japan), Guangdong TV (China), Rogers Sportsnet (Canada), TDS (Curacao) and RPC (Panama) were all on-site to provide live commentary and news feeds to their home countries.

"We try to make the broadcast as universal as possible," said Russell Gabay, vice president and executive producer of international operations for MLB. "Thorne's and Sutcliffe's challenge is keeping their commentary basic enough to educate new fans, while still making it compelling for experienced viewers. We know we are dealing with dozens of different cultures and customs, and we have to produce with those differences in mind. It is a much more complex undertaking than a single-country production."

No matter where fans live, the All-Star Game is perfect for international audiences because so many of the players are foreign-born. As a result, Gabay has learned to alter the broadcast to give those viewers exactly what they want — as many shots of their homeland heroes as possible.

"We know the iconic stature of these players in their home markets. Because of that, when Albert Pujols comes up to bat, we will make sure that he gets camera time for his fans in the Dominican Republic," he said. "If Ichiro is in the box and steps out, we go with that rather than following the foul ball he hit. Fans want to follow their local heroes."

While Fox uses its own crew to broadcast the game to a predominantly domestic audience, Major League Baseball International (MLBI) produces an ad-free worldwide feed of the All-Star showcase. MLBI utilizes its own team to customize the audio and video for rightsholders across the globe. The international production uses eight cameras.

WORLD-RENOWNED Perennial All-Star Albert Pujols has become a cultural phenomenon across the globe.

UNITED NATIONS
Dominican-born Hanley
Ramirez and Japan-born
Ichiro Suzuki have caused
quite a stir abroad with
their All-Star selections.

CAUGHT LOOKING A staple on the American League All-Star team from 2005–07, Venezuela native Johan Santana has an extensive following in his home country.

CREDENTIALS

More reporters cover All-Star Week than any other MLB event, and the league's public relations team shoulders the credential requests from around the country — and in some cases, the world. John Blundell, who coordinates the process from MLB's office in New York, launches the online credential application in April.

Ultimately, more than 3,000 credentials are issued for the event, split between media, rightsholders and MLB staff and officials. While some credentials grant access for the entire stretch of All-Star Week, others are specific to just one of the three days. Sunday, with the XM All-Star Futures Game and the Taco Bell All-Star Legends & Celebrity Softball Game, is light on national media presence, drawing a larger number of Minor League and entertainment reporters; Monday and Tuesday are bigger media draws.

Year to year, Blundell's group sees little variation in the number of credential requests. "All-Star is pretty consistent," he said. "It's on the schedule for years, so it's easy to plan how to get there. The World Series can be a lot harder for some media outlets to get to on short notice." The home market, though, always requests the most credentials, with everyone from the team's beat writers to the local government reporters needing to cover what is a major civic event.

Over time, the credentials have evolved significantly, from the pins of the All-Star Game's early years to today's plastic badges, which feature a photo of the credential-holder and holograms for security purposes.

PRESS PINS

Of all the All-Star collectibles, press pins are among the most sought after. The original press credentials, pins don't serve any official purpose today, but their unique design and limited quantities — about 6,000 each year — make them popular with fans.

Each year, every member of MLB's design services department submits a design, which is then die-cast, and MLB staffers vote for the winner. For the All-Star Game, an effort is made to include some unique, interactive elements. Recent years have seen a working compass on the 2001 pin for the game in Seattle, a ball falling into San Francisco Bay in 2007, dirt from Yankee Stadium in '08, and a star dangling from a chain for the 2010 contest in Anaheim.

PRESS BOXES

With more than 3,000 credentials issued for All-Star Week, the task of finding a place to put everyone once the game starts can be an ordeal. That job falls to John Blundell, MLB's manager of media relations, who controls the approximately 600 tabletop seats that are split between the stadium's main press box and the auxiliary press box, a section of seats in the stadium reserved for media and outfitted with outlets, televisions and desks.

Most stadiums have about 100–125 seats in their main boxes, which is plenty for a regular-season game but not nearly enough for the media crush that accompanies an All-Star Game. Designating seats for the auxiliary box, which is assembled by local carpenters contracted by MLB, is always a balance between getting good seats and views for the members of the media, who will have to write about the games, without taking too many prime viewing areas away from the fans.

Blundell is in charge of the seating chart for each of the week's marquee events, and he plots it by adhering to a rotation of the major news sources. First, he gives prime spots to the home market's newspapers, which usually get the best seats in both the main and auxiliary boxes because of the local hype the game generates. They're followed by major news wires, such as The Associated Press. Next come any traveling papers, which he tries to group together, placing, for example, Chicago writers next to one another where possible. After that come newspapers that cover only home games, followed by national sports media entities — *Sports Illustrated*, ESPN — and then non-baseball periodicals and radio reporters.

In the press boxes, MLB's public relations staffers distribute press notes filled with stats and pieces of information that the reporters can use in stories. They also announce in-game milestones, such as when David Wright extended his All-Star Game hitting streak to five games in 2010, and the many lineup changes that take place during the course of the contest. Others in the press box include members of the Baseball Writers Association of America, as well as the designated official scorers, who rule on errors and wild pitches. The auxiliary box is wired with speakers so that reporters can hear the same announcements.

PROGRAMS

When it comes to timeless souvenirs from the All-Star Game, it's tough to top the *Official All-Star Game Program*. The publication weighs in at more than 250 pages and includes feature stories, a history of the Midsummer Classic, team rosters and an oversized scorecard suited to fit the names of the 60-plus players who will take the field. As with the game programs for MLB's other jewel events, the *Official All-Star Game Program* is produced by MLB's internal publishing group.

In addition to designing a cover for the program that speaks to the host city, as well as another cover that features a current star from the host team, MLB began printing covers that feature one All-Star from each club in 2007. "The *Official All-Star Game Program Limited Player Edition* books afford fans the opportunity to celebrate their favorite teams and those players who are participating in the Midsummer Classic," said Don Hintze, MLB's vice president of publishing and photos. "The *Official All-Star Game Program* represents the historic significance of the event long after the final out is recorded, and these limited editions will evoke special memories about the teams and players involved."

The history of the souvenir program goes all the way back to the initial Midsummer Classic, debuting in 1933. Fans attending that inaugural contest at Chicago's Comiskey Park could purchase a program for 10 cents, and the cover boasted a huge advertisement for Blue Valley Butter.

Today, the program isn't just available to the lucky folks at the game. It can also be found at retail outlets throughout the host city and at All-Star FanFest. And, thanks to MLB.com, fans are just a few clicks away from ordering their very own official program even if they're far from the action.

Each year's All-Star program is filled with stories written by the nation's top baseball scribes, including Tim Kurkjian, Jayson Stark and George F. Will. MLB's publishing team assembles its editorial lineup and doles out assignments to writers in February and March. In April, as manuscripts are submitted and edited, the design and photo teams help determine the program's creative direction. By May, production is in full swing, and by late June, the bulk of the book is printed. In early July — right after the TBS *All-Star Selection Show* — game rosters are added once the All-Stars are named. Within hours, the last stage of printing and binding is complete, and the souvenirs are shipped to the All-Star Game site.

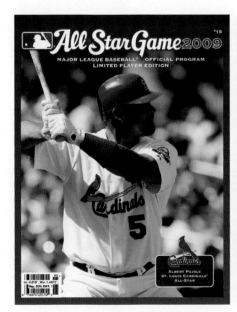

PLAYBILLS The *Official All-Star Game Program* is a coveted collectible each year.

PHOTOS

Fans at any of the All-Star Week events seem to constantly be jockeying for position, willing to do whatever it takes to get as close to the action as possible. Luckily for the professional photographers on hand to document the festivities, they already own the most coveted spots.

The talented men and women who descend on the host site to capture the indelible images of All-Star Week take a vastly different approach to their work than they do during the regular season. It should come as no surprise that many news organizations want to be perfectly in position for every event, ready to photograph iconic images from the Home Run Derby and the All-Star Game itself. But in keeping with the lighthearted nature of the Midsummer Classic, many photographers find themselves focused on the spontaneity and emotion of the week. Receiving some All-Star treatment of their own, photographers are permitted on the field during the ancillary events. Unlike regular-season assignments, photographers are looking to capture All-Stars interacting with their teammates and families, as players often do during the Derby. During All-Star festivities, it's casual images like these that are just as important, if not more so, than the action taking place between the lines.

The contingent of photographers at the All-Star Game is yet another diversion from a typical game scenario. While a regular-season contest often attracts just eight to 10 photographers — who position themselves in sunken camera "wells" adjacent to the dugouts — that number can swell to about six times that size during All-Star Week events. Such was the case in Anaheim in 2010, when more than 60 photography credentials were issued. Photographers from the host city generally receive the most credentials, as All-Star Week festivities drive local news coverage. Team photographers also abound, chronicling the All-Star representatives from their respective clubs throughout the week. Major news organizations and wire services, as well as MLB photographers, round out the contingent of cameras.

Mingling with players on the field and fans throughout the host city, MLB photographers cover everything on the All-Star calendar, beginning with All-Star FanFest, continuing into the Futures Game and Legends & Celebrity Softball Game on Sunday; running through All-Star Workout Day and the Home Run Derby on Monday, and finally onto the red carpet for a parade before the game on Tuesday. During batting practice, MLB photographers and runners can be found dodging baseballs in the outfield while setting up lights and risers for the team photos. Once batting practice ends, they attempt to organize the players — who are sometimes more interested in reuniting with former teammates than the flashbulbs — for team photos.

And that's just on the field. Moving indoors, a studio that can be used for formal portraits is set up inside the ballpark. Players are urged to document the event with their families, and some even use the photos on their holiday cards. Cameras are also permitted in the media availability sessions and press conferences — which in recent years have been dressed by MLB's design services team to make for better images — and photographers certainly take advantage.

CANDID CAMERA
Unlike the regular season, photographers primarily focus on taking candid shots during All-Star Week.

CHAPTER 5: MONDAY

So, it's All-Star Monday. The Minor League stars' moment in the sun has passed with the conclusion of Sunday's Futures Game, and all of the Major League honorees have finally convened in the host city. With just one full day separating fans from baseball's marquee midsummer event, there's no time to waste; a full schedule of events lies ahead and there are many opportunities to take advantage of. Reporters clamor for access to players during the morning's media sessions and press conferences, with MLB public relations personnel ensuring that everything runs according to plan — the cameras, after all, are rolling. The All-Stars then head to the field for mid-afternoon batting practice, when they gather with their entire team for the first time. A smooth transition into the evening's festivities makes sure that the Home Run Derby — one of All-Star Week's most popular draws for fans, Big Leaguers and their families, alike — goes off without a hitch. And what a show it is.

WORLD ON HIS SHOULDERS Victor Martinez gave his son a great view of the action at the 2007 Home Run Derby in San Francisco.

DERBY DAY

IT'S HARD TO SAY EXACTLY WHEN THE HOME RUN DERBY turned into the extravaganza that devoured All-Star Monday. But make no mistake — we're now living in a world in which more Americans tune in to ESPN to watch sluggers like Vladimir Guerrero launch a batting practice fastball into a kayak than to see an NBA playoff game.

"The Derby is the most watched cable sports event of the summer," said Tim Brosnan, executive vice president, business, for Major League Baseball. "The spectacle of a baseball flying off into the night — it's a great show in person and on television."

But the coolest thing about the Derby is that the most feared sluggers in the world get so amped up for it. Red Sox designated hitter David Ortiz won in 2010, and recent years have seen unforgettable performances from All-Stars such as Guerrero, Josh Hamilton, Bobby Abreu, Prince Fielder, Ryan Howard and many others. "It's one of those things that doesn't lose its luster," said five-time AL All-Star Frank Thomas, twice a Derby participant. "The Home Run Derby, people get stoked for every year. And every year you've got two or three new guys who are breakout stars who put their names on the map."

The Phillies' Howard was one of those up-and-coming new guys in '06, blasting 23 home runs into the Pittsburgh ozone — six of which splashed into the Allegheny River behind PNC Park — winning one fan a house and securing another fan 500 free flights, thanks to promotions tied to the event. In three magical hours, Howard became a household name on the way to a monstrous second half and MVP recognition.

Of course, it's difficult to imagine any player breaking out during a Derby more than Hamilton did during Yankee Stadium's last hurrah in 2008. That night, he sent 28 first-round shots into the old ballpark's seats, eclipsing Abreu's single-round record of 24 — set in 2005 in Detroit — and enrapturing those watching in the stadium and at home. It was a performance that may never be matched.

It's hard to believe that when the Derby began back in 1985, it was an afterthought stuffed between NL and AL batting practices to raise money for an amateur baseball charity. Nobody televised it. Hardly anybody wrote about it. It's safe to say the event has since gained a little more attention. Darryl Strawberry first turned heads, bashing a homer off an Astrodome speaker in 1986. But it took until 1991 for the Derby to begin its ascent toward cultural event status. Cal Ripken Jr. pumped a then-record 12 home runs to win that year, but Cecil Fielder was the highlight machine, whomping two balls into the bar in the third deck in center field at Toronto's SkyDome.

VLADIMIR THE GREAT
Vladimir Guerrero launched 17 homers in one evening to take the 2007 Derby trophy.

HOW FAR IT'S COME
Ryan Howard, the
2006 Home Run Derby
champ, made his mark
by hitting 23 longballs
during the event.

FIELD DAY

Unlike the All-Star Game, which follows the natural rhythms of a baseball game, the Home Run Derby is full of action and activity. So what better way to get the party started than with a mini rock concert on the field?

ESPN cameras go live as a pre-Derby musical act plays on a stage around second base, with fireworks in the background and All-Star Game banners on the speakers. In 2010, the Grammy Award–winning band Train performed in Anaheim, inviting fans inside to the sounds of their hit song "Hey, Soul Sister." Just before going live, MLB Network showed the band playing its 2003 hit "Calling All Angels" — an appropriate choice considering the setting, and one welcomed enthusiastically in the ballpark.

MLB works with record labels, band managers and agents to coordinate performances, identifying interested bands and finding acts that will resonate in the local markets and on TV. Scheduling can be an obstacle, due to tours or studio recording schedules, but most musical acts are very interested in an opportunity like this.

The first truly spectacular Derby field, assembled in San Diego in 1992, featured Ripken, Ken Griffey Jr., Barry Bonds, Joe Carter, Mark McGwire, Larry Walker, Fred McGriff and a young Gary Sheffield. Then came '94 at Three Rivers Stadium in Pittsburgh, where Griffey crunched five balls into the upper deck on as many straight swings. And Thomas squashed the longest ball ever hit there — a 519-foot lunar orbiter. It was such a momentous blast that the Pirates put a star on the upper-deck seat where it landed, and then had Thomas and Dodgers coach Rich Donnelly, who threw the pitch, sign the star, auctioning it off before they demolished the stadium in 2001.

The Derby took a dramatic leap forward in 1996 when Bonds out-slugged McGwire at Veterans Stadium. And it cemented its status in '99, when McGwire smoked 5,692 feet worth of home runs off light towers, parking garages and lobster pots all over Boston. More than a decade later, it's impossible to forget that night, because to many, Derby memories are now just about as indelible as memories of All-Star Games themselves.

And not just for the players, either. The Derby has developed a huge charitable focus, thanks to the help of the event's title sponsor, State Farm, which, together with MLB, donated $573,000 during the 2010 event. In addition to the use of gold balls — thrown when a player is down to his last out — which raise money for charity when a player hits a homer with one, State Farm also assists local Boys & Girls Clubs by pairing each competitor in the Derby with a kid from a local chapter. During the 2010 event, State Farm donated $10,000 to the club of each competitor's matched child, with an extra $40,000 going to Boys & Girls Clubs of Fullerton, Calif., as a youngster named Malik Campbell rode Ortiz's success to the championship. Over the first four years that State Farm sponsored the Home Run Derby, it partnered with MLB to donate more than $1.7 million to help create big moments for Boys & Girls Clubs of America and its local chapters.

The charitable efforts are the finishing touches on an event that thrills fans every time. With players hanging out on the field with their families and recording video, the atmosphere is like nothing else during the season. Some players agree to be miked up or interviewed on the field, and unlike regular-season games, when the ancillary entertainment is reserved for those watching on TV, those in the park get to hear everything, too.

FAMILY GUY
Brad Hawpe, like many All-Stars, had his kids in tow for the 2009 Home Run Derby in St. Louis.

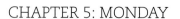

Although all eyes are on the field, the tidal wave of fan enthusiasm can be a powerful force. Howard had one out remaining in the first round in '06, needing four straight homers to stay alive. Next thing he knew, the crowd was roaring, he found his stroke and baseballs started soaring into the river flowing behind Pittsburgh's PNC Park.

Granted, you're not winning any Derbies if you don't whale away. But in 2002, after hitting just one homer in his first contest, Houston's Lance Berkman reached an important conclusion: Swinging can be overrated, too.

"After my first time," Berkman said, "one of my buddies said, 'Were you in the Home Run Derby? I never saw you.' I said, 'That's because I was gone in about five-and-a-half minutes.'"

So his next time, Berkman planned on taking a few pitches. It worked so well, he made it to the 2004 finals. Brosnan recalls being in the home clubhouse at PNC Park before the 2006 Derby when a sweat-soaked Berkman came in from the batting cage and took newcomers Howard and David Wright aside to talk strategy.

"His [Lance Berkman's] message was, 'Don't exhaust yourself in the first round because I've seen too many guys go crazy in the first round and they're out of gas in the second,'" Brosnan said. "Then we went in the other clubhouse, and David Ortiz was pumped up from winning. He came out that night ready to go. They're all like prize fighters before the fight. This is about competing. This is about their pride."

GOLD BASEBALLS

It may seem as though players invited to participate in the Home Run Derby have been given a golden ticket to one of baseball's most esteemed events. But the real riches can be found in a recent Midsummer Classic initiative — gold baseballs. Introduced during the 2005 Home Run Derby, the gold balls are designed by Rawlings and are used in every round of the contest. They're not thrown until a batter is down to his final out and then they are tossed as long as he stays alive in the round. Each home run that a player hits with one is worth approximately $20,000 in charitable donations to organizations such as Boys & Girls Clubs of America and Easter Seals.

A total of 28 homers — 14 each in 2005 and '06 — were hit in the first two gold-ball years. That number was rivaled in Anaheim in 2010, when Derby participants launched 12 golden longballs. Since the gold ball's All-Star debut, these extra-special home runs have generated nearly $2 million for charity through MLB and its sponsors.

RECORD KEEPING
All-Stars like the Red Sox's Jason Varitek, who brought his daughter to New York in 2008, never want to forget the experience.

CLASSIC LONGBALLS

BASEBALL'S SLUGGERS CERTAINLY HAVEN'T RELEGATED LONG-balls to the Home Run Derby. From the very first All-Star homer by Babe Ruth in 1933 to game-winning blasts from Stan Musial, Ted Williams, Johnny Callison and Hank Blalock over the years, plenty of towering hits have left the stadium during the contest.

Williams, for one, launched two home runs during Midsummer Classic action, his second coming in 1946 on an eephus pitch from Rip Sewell — the only Big League blast ever off the unique pitch.

Even though he's known as "Mr. October," Reggie Jackson had no trouble rocketing a memorable pitch into the July sky in Detroit in 1971. According to calculations by one physics professor, the ball would have traveled 510 feet if it hadn't struck a transformer on the roof of Tiger Stadium.

Until Fred Lynn came to the plate more than a decade later in 1983, 119 All-Star Game homers had been hit, with nary a grand slam among them. His blast into the right-field bleachers at Comiskey Park is the only bases-loaded bomb in All-Star Game history.

Two-sport marvel Bo Jackson waited a few more years before rivaling Reggie's mammoth roundtripper in 1989. Batting leadoff for the first time in his career, Jackson launched a 448-foot rocket to dead center field in Anaheim Stadium that, in the words of the *Los Angeles Times*, "punched a hole in the sky."

THE NATURAL

AT RANGERS BALLPARK IN ARLINGTON, MOONSHOTS BY THE home team are heralded with the iconic theme music from *The Natural*. But most fans watching the Home Run Derby at Yankee Stadium on July 14, 2008, didn't know that yet. What they did know was that this kid, Josh Hamilton, was essentially starring in his own personal remake of the Robert Redford classic.

As the top overall pick in the 1999 First-Year Player Draft, Hamilton was a sure-thing prospect whose career nearly ended before it started, with injuries keeping him off the field and his personal life spiraling into a mess of drug and alcohol abuse. Out of baseball for years, he made his way back with the Reds in 2007 and was traded to the Rangers before the '08 season. Over the next few years, Hamilton would establish himself as a regular at the All-Star Game, even winning the AL MVP Award in 2010. But the night of the Home Run Derby in 2008, as he crushed one monstrous home run after another, Hamilton stamped his ticket to stardom in front of one of the biggest audiences he will ever play in front of. And wouldn't you know it, at one point during the barrage, the Yankee Stadium public address system began playing *The Natural* theme.

"I think it was just a chance for everyone to see what we see all the time," said Michael Young, Hamilton's teammate in Texas and a fellow 2008 All-Star. "That's a testament not only to Josh's ability as a player but the magnetism he has as far as to really transcend the game. You know you talk about players who played a long time ago. Players in the years ahead are going to look at Josh and say, 'That's a guy I want to play like,' because he can do everything so well on the field."

The serendipitous connection to the epic baseball movie with uncanny similarities to Hamilton's own life got even better the next day. After returning to his hotel room at about 12:30 once the Derby finished and eating a room service dinner, Hamilton finally got to sleep around 3 a.m. When he woke up six hours later, he flipped on the TV to find — what else — *The Natural* playing on TV.

"I turn on one channel and the end of the movie is on, right before he's about to hit the home run," Hamilton said in the clubhouse before that year's All-Star Game. "Someone knocked on the door and came in and sat down, and I said, 'Hold on, I gotta see this.' So we sat and watched it."

As the top overall pick in the 1999 First-Year Player Draft, Hamilton was a sure-thing prospect whose career nearly ended before it started. But the night of the Home Run Derby in 2008, as he crushed one monstrous home run after another, Hamilton stamped his ticket to stardom in front of one of the biggest audiences he will ever play in front of.

GRANDEUR
Representing the Angels in the 1983 affair, Fred Lynn hit the only grand slam in Midsummer Classic history.

NATURAL STROKE
Josh Hamilton propelled a record 28 first-round shots into the Yankee Stadium seats during the 2008 Home Run Derby.

PITCHER PERFECT

ARMS RACE
Ken Griffey Jr. triumphed in the '99
Derby with Clint Hurdle on the mound.

*Manager Clint Hurdle recalls his unexpected role at the 1999
Home Run Derby when he threw to four different guys.*

Although the Derby was still in its early stages, it was a nice dynamic at Fenway. But then you get out on the mound, where you're checking everything out. Throwing batting practice is one thing; throwing in front of 39,000 people in the stands — and something like 9 million more watching on TV — is another. They remove the cage, which creates a whole different visual than I'm used to. And the media attention is something of a carnival, so you've got a few different emotions going that you normally don't have for BP in the afternoon.

I was there to throw to Larry Walker. Normally, you throw 50 mph. That night I wanted to be firm. My job was to make it easy on Larry, let him hit home runs — something every pitcher in the league was doing just fine that year. Nobody could get him out that season. Nobody — except me. I ended up eliminating him in the first round. And I was his batting practice pitcher!

So I walked off the mound feeling pretty bad for Larry, and I figured, "Well, I'm good. I'm done. Didn't embarrass myself or hurt anyone. Now I'll go shower, grab my wife and we'll go to the parties and actually try to have some fun."

Then Jeromy Burnitz walks over. He's a player I had in the Minors with the Mets. Jeromy had a guy come with him, but he was too nervous to throw. So Jeromy asked if I'd throw to him. I shook my head, thinking, "I had him as a Minor Leaguer. He's in the Big Leagues now. I can't say no."

Well, Jeromy's bombing the ball off to the right and I got in a better groove. I got my breath back and relaxed a little bit more. He hits a bunch of homers. We walk off and it looks like he might be in position to move forward.

Then I get a tap on the shoulder, and it's Jeff Bagwell. "Hey," he said. "I don't have a guy to throw. Would you mind throwing to me?" I thought, "Jeez, that's like another trip to the dentist's office." But out of professional respect for Jeff, and since I was there anyway, I said, "Well, sure, I'll throw." And he bombed — in a good way. So I'm walking off, thinking, "Wow, looks like I might have a couple guys moving on."

Then I get another tap on the shoulder, and it's somebody representing Ken Griffey Jr. asking if I would throw to him. Now I'm like, "Holy cow, wait a minute. This is the fourth guy I'm going to throw to this round." It's a lengthy event. But Griffey Jr. — we're not messing around — this is the cherry on top of the sundae. I'd better throw good, but do I want to accept this responsibility? I thought, "Well, I'm already in. We'll see where this goes." So he hits a bunch of homers. Well, sonofagun, I have three guys going to the second round. So I throw and throw and throw. It turns out that Burnitz and Griffey are in the finals — both mine! So we have to reset the trap and do it all again. In the end, Griffey won, 3-2.

I had to figure out what these guys liked quickly. You're trying to move it forward, and they're giving you directions. They're looking for one particular pitch. So as the night went on, I was just as fatigued mentally as I was physically.

They play it on ESPN Classic now, so I always get a few comments. I watched it one time. It was fun to see. Normally if you put a Home Run Derby on, you're watching the kid hitting. But I'm saying, "No, no — watch! I'm the guy throwing. I'm the pitcher who finally figured out how to beat Larry Walker."

ATTENTION GRABBER
All eyes — and microphones — were on AL hurler Dan Haren when he was tabbed to start the 2007 contest.

MEDIA

ON THE MONDAY BEFORE THE 2009 ALL-STAR GAME, ZACH DUKE and Freddy Sanchez were sitting at a table in the Regency Ballroom at the Hyatt Regency St. Louis Riverfront hotel. The two Pirates teammates were waiting for the start of the NL media availability — and Sanchez sensed that his tablemate might not have been prepared for what was in store.

"You're not going to believe what's going to happen when the doors open," Sanchez, then in his third Midsummer Classic, told first-timer Duke.

MLB issued 2,836 credentials to the '09 All-Star Game, but the horde of reporters who elbow, kick and shove their way into the two media availability sessions sometimes seems five times that size. With all of the players seated at tables in a single room — the big stars alone, the All-Stars who draw lighter crowds doubling up — the 50-minute sessions are the most fruitful opportunities for press to secure interviews to use in All-Star coverage and beyond.

Before the 1999 game, All-Star media sessions were similar to those during the regular season — reporters would seek players in the clubhouses. But there simply wasn't enough room in the cramped clubhouses at Fenway Park to handle the media crush at the '99 Midsummer Classic. To accommodate the throng that would have been unimaginable when Fenway opened in 1912, MLB brought the players and reporters together in a ballroom at Boston's Westin Copley Place hotel. The idea worked so well that it stuck. And these days, with more cameras in the room and MLB Network providing live coverage, the sessions have become an event in their own right.

"It used to be mostly radio and print at the media availability," said Anne Occi, MLB's vice president of design services. "You didn't have to dress up the room. Now with all the cameras, it all has to look better." To that end, Occi's team decks out the room in black curtains, with bunting wrapping the tables, which are positioned on risers. The players' names appear on signs above their heads and are printed on a gray background so as not to reflect light from cameras.

The host league's players are available first, with players from the host team — like Albert Pujols in St. Louis — given prime spots because of the local attention they generate. The biggest stars also get mobbed. In the mid-2000s, Barry Bonds' table was so crushed that the seating plan made sure that he was next to players who drew lighter crowds. Generally, each team's players are grouped together for the beat writers' convenience, with national writers moving to pick up a quote here or a comment there. Some reporters camp out at one table the whole session; if you don't get to a superstar like Alex Rodriguez in the first minute, good luck getting close in the next 49.

For the players, most of whom fly into town after their games on Sunday, often landing late at night and sometimes early Monday morning, the media sessions are the first public All-Star activity, following a private brunch for All-Stars and their families. And while sitting at a table surrounded by microphones might not be the highlight of the week, it does allow players to fulfill most of their media obligations in a quick period. "There's a pretty good template we have for it at this point," said MLB PR Manager Mike Teevan. "You want it to be a good experience for the players and their families, so you want to make sure you give them some time to be together and enjoy the week."

PUBLIC RELATIONS

Major League Baseball's public relations team spends almost a full year preparing for the All-Star Game. And by the time each Midsummer Classic rolls around, after months of planning and nearly a week of ancillary events, one thought is pretty common in the PR office at the staff hotel: "Thank God Monday is over."

As any MLB PR staffer will tell you, All-Star Monday is the longest day of the year, beginning with press conferences and media availability in the staff hotel, moving to the ballpark for batting practice, and concluding with the State Farm Home Run Derby. No matter how much attention the rest of the baseball-loving world might focus on Tuesday night's All-Star Game, it's nothing compared to what MLB PR Manager Mike Teevan and his team have survived before the first pitch.

Media planning for the All-Star Game begins in February, when MLB's 25-person PR team — including various club PR directors who help out every year — descends on the host city to scout the stadium. While in town, the staffers designate seating sections for the auxiliary press box, allocate parking for broadcast trucks, reserve media hotels and things of that nature. "It's easy in Anaheim because of two things: They have extensive postseason experience, and Angels VP of Communications Tim Mead is one of the best in the business," Teevan said in 2010. "The Angels are always good about taking care of the media and being accessible."

> *All-Star Monday is the longest day of the year, beginning with press conferences and media availability, moving to the ballpark for BP, and concluding with the Home Run Derby.*

In April, the big All-Star ticketing push begins, although FanFest ticket sales begin earlier. MLB works with local ambassadors, usually one current star and one team legend from the host city — in 2009, it was Ozzie Smith and Albert Pujols — to build buzz around the city before the game. Also in April, the ballot is unveiled and MLB's community relations team begins its quest to promote charitable events over the course of the entire summer.

Once the balloting begins, things quiet down for the PR group until the All-Stars are announced around July 4 weekend — and then the action picks up again. Immediately after the All-Star rosters are revealed, Teevan and crew get to work finishing the All-Star Media Guide, a 240-page book which focuses 70 pages on the All-Star teams. The guide is finished the night the All-Stars are named, and the PR group travels to the host city the next day. On site, Teevan is almost always at the stadium or media hotel, coordinating everything from the notes given to reporters before each event to the large scale media availability on All-Star Monday.

It all builds up to Tuesday. "But by that point," Teevan said, "it's really a regular game in a lot of ways."

Although All-Star travel is more predictable, the whole experience is more exhausting than the postseason, which is almost entirely focused on the field. "The buildup is huge," Teevan said. "And the event keeps growing."

TALK TIME

In addition to the free-ranging scrums during media availability on All-Star Monday, the day is also full of formal press conferences, which take place at the MLB staff hotel. The first, which usually begins early in the morning, features the managers of both leagues on a dais, alongside the leagues' honorary presidents — Jackie Autry for the AL and Bill Giles for the NL. During the course of the session, which is broadcast live on MLB Network, the managers name their starting pitchers — who also sit at the dais — and present their starting lineups. The highlight of recent press conferences came when Autry would poke fun at her NL counterpart's significant winless streak, which began in 1997 before finally ending in Anaheim in 2010. In 2008, Autry, the wife of former Angels Owner and legendary "Singing Cowboy" Gene, told the media that she "went to church and said a novena for Bill Giles."

Next on the dais are the eight participants in that night's Home Run Derby. The mood during the press conference, like the Derby itself, is always light, with the contestants opening up about everything from strategy in the batter's box to how they would celebrate if they won. "I want all these guys to carry me off the field," Arizona's Chris Young said during the 2010 press conference.

CENTER STAGE
Named the AL starting pitcher in 2010,
David Price fielded reporters' questions.

DAVID PRICE

PRACTICE MAKES PERFECT

BEFORE THE ESPN CAMERAS TURN ON TO SHOWCASE THE Home Run Derby on All-Star Monday, the stands fill up with fans wanting to catch a glimpse of Gatorade All-Star Workout Day, when the All-Stars take the field together for the first time, wearing specially designed All-Star batting practice jerseys and swinging in one of the most visible batting practice sessions of their careers.

MLB Network broadcasts the workout, showing the players as they take cuts in the cage and hang out on the field. It's a loose event and the first time the All-Stars assemble between the lines in any given year. "It's a time to come out and just kind of unwind a little bit, have a good time," said Ryan Howard. "It's about interacting with the guys and getting out on the field and taking in all of the festivities."

But the Big League All-Stars aren't the only ones who get to take some cuts on the field during All-Star Week; top MLB clients also get the chance to swing for the fences. Every year, MLB coordinates a client batting practice for its corporate partners. The casual event takes place in the morning, and clients shag flies, hang out on the field and tour the ballpark — including the clubhouses. In Anaheim during 2010 All-Star Week, former Angels hurler Chuck Finley threw batting practice, with each client getting about eight swings.

SOUVENIRS

FEW FANS GO TO THE ALL-STAR GAME WITHOUT TAKING A piece of it home. And MLB's licensees make sure that everyone in attendance during All-Star Week has plenty of options when shopping for souvenirs.

There are bats engraved with the Midsummer Classic logo that you can choose to personalize, T-shirts with a name and number for each All-Star, bobblehead dolls and Phiten titanium necklaces. Any baseball accoutrement that you can imagine is offered — and stamped with the official All-Star Game logo specific to that year's event. Along with The Sports Authority, the official retail partner of All-Star FanFest, MLB organizes a massive retail operation at Fan-Fest, but fans can find officially licensed All-Star products all over the host city every time the game rolls into town. The league's licensees always try to create something special for each event.

In recent years, MLB has promoted the All-Star Week festivities by placing themed statues — Statues of Liberty in New York, Gateway Arches in St. Louis and Mickey Mouses in Anaheim — around the host city. The statues are decked out with All-Star logos, as well as designs for all 30 teams and both leagues. No surprise, smaller, replica versions of the statues are some of the best-selling keepsakes during the week. Also popular in 2010 were items from MLB's retail partnership with Victoria's Secret PINK. At FanFest in Anaheim, the PINK items sold out in one day. And there's always a huge market for customized items, too, such as All-Star jerseys personalized with a fan's name.

As part of their agreements with Major League Baseball, all of the licensees are authorized to use the logos for the Midsummer Classic on any product related to the event — a stance not taken in every sport. And they certainly take advantage. "Everyone wants in for the All-Star Game market," said Greg Sim, MLB Properties' senior director of licensing.

There are also plenty of All-Star souvenirs that a fan can receive just by walking into the ballpark. Anyone attending the week's festivities in recent years has received free giveaways — from ticket holders and lanyards at Taco Bell All-Star Sunday and Gatorade All-Star Workout Day on Monday to drawstring bags and seat cushions filled with coupon offers at the All-Star Game — all bearing the event logos, of course. And that's not even mentioning one of the most sought-after souvenirs of all — a ticket stub from an All-Star Week event.

But for all of the unique items that attract the attention of crowds who flock to sporting goods stores just before and during All-Star Week, the standard baseball trappings remain in demand. "Jerseys, tees and caps are always the most popular items each year," said Adam Blinderman, MLB's senior director, consumer products–retail marketing. Countless fans seek out the All-Star jersey of their favorite player or caps with Midsummer Classic logos heat-pressed onto the side. Another on-field item that is a hot commodity and is considered a classic collectible is an official Rawlings All-Star Game baseball. You don't even have to catch it!

WHALE AWAY
All-Star Ichiro Suzuki fine-tuned his stroke during 2009 Gatorade All-Star Workout Day.

PARTNERSHIPS

ALL-STAR WEEK IS A PRIME BUSINESS OPPORTUNITY FOR MAJOR LEAGUE BASEBALL'S MOST important partners. A key element of the partnership between MLB and its corporate sponsors comes from creating unique marketing platforms and finding the most innovative ways to integrate their brands. The Midsummer Classic provides great exposure, from Taco Bell All-Star Sunday, featuring the XM All-Star Futures Game and the Taco Bell All-Star Legends & Celebrity Softball Game, to Gatorade All-Star Workout Day on Monday with its jewel, the State Farm Home Run Derby.

"Each year, our partners join us to make All-Star Week one of the premier events in all of sports," said Tim Brosnan, executive vice president, business, for MLB. "From events at the ballpark to All-Star FanFest exhibits and community projects, the festivities that surround All-Star provide our sponsors great exposure, while the sponsor participation lets us take the All-Star experience to fans both inside and outside the ballpark."

Not only do sponsors help make the events possible, but they try to add to the fans' experience, as well. Many fans are interested in preserving their tickets and other mementos from these events for posterity, so sponsors often provide anyone who enters the gates with giveaways, such as ticket holders and lanyards. And that's just the beginning — in 2009, as part of MLB's partnership with Anheuser-Busch, the famed Budweiser Clydesdales took the field before the All-Star Game.

During All-Star Week, MLB's design services department, led by Anne Occi, ensures that the sponsors' logos pop both on TV and in the stadium. The process begins when Occi's team works with the sponsorship group to scout the host stadium and identify the best spots for signage. Making it all look great is a huge task, one that requires late nights throughout All-Star Week. Occi's team installs the signage for all three days at one time, layering each level on top of the one for the next night to lessen the workload somewhat. That allows them to remove the Taco Bell and XM materials after Sunday to reveal the Gatorade and State Farm signs already in place for Monday. It helps, but with events running late into the night, particularly on the East Coast, it remains a considerable amount of work.

BIG SHOT A giant baseball in McCovey Cove promoted 2007 All-Star Monday's main event.

ALL-STAR TEAM
Budweiser's famed Clydesdales
visited Busch Stadium in '09.

CHAPTER 6:
ON WITH THE SHOW

FIRST-TIME MIDSUMMER CLASSIC ATTENDEES WOULD BE MAKING A MAJOR mistake if they arrived in town just for the All-Star Game on Tuesday. Over the years, the event has grown from a nine-inning exhibition into an extravaganza known as All-Star Week, where there is just as much to do away from the field as there is to see on it. Even those without tickets to the marquee event can get in on the All-Star fun by attending All-Star FanFest, a one-of-a-kind trade show and fan convention. The All-Star Gala and Pregame Party are both key components of the social scene that help make the week's festivities a hip scene. Of course, once fans make their way into the ballpark, there is no shortage of bells and whistles before the game begins. From pop superstars singing the national anthem moments before military jets fly over the ballpark to special pregame events like the emotional introductions of the All-Century Team or a first pitch by a sitting U.S. president, it's a blockbuster before the game even starts.

STAGE DELIGHT *Glee*'s Amber Riley traded the high school stage for a national one when she sang the national anthem before the 2010 game.

HAVING A BALL
Each year, All-Star
FanFest showcases the
World's Largest Baseball.

ALL-STAR SHOWCASE

It's the largest baseball fan event in the world, and, as you might imagine, it's quite a production. Every year during All-Star Week, MLB All-Star FanFest opens the festivities in the host city on the Friday before the game, days before the players even arrive. FanFest is part industry trade show, with baseball equipment manufacturers displaying the newest hardball wares; part baseball festival, with games and food; and part Hall of Fame roadshow, where fans can see selections from the vast collection of memorabilia at Cooperstown. The fan-centric event also features interactive exhibits and attractions, clinics and seminars, autograph sessions, memorabilia sales, and anything else baseball-related you can imagine.

The five-day extravaganza is a family-friendly event with activities and displays to please fans of all ages, bursting at the seams with a passion for baseball. With tickets to in-stadium All-Star Week events scarce, FanFest is designed to allow generations of baseball fans to share in the once-in-a-lifetime experience when a Midsummer Classic comes to town. "We try to show the game of baseball from multiple angles," said Jackie Secaira-Cotto, MLB's director of special events, who runs the whole FanFest operation. "We want to have the kids and families see the game in different ways and learn something new."

FanFest is a big party, one that occupied 450,000 square feet at the Anaheim Convention Center in 2010 and welcomed more than 100,000 fans, who spent an average of four hours there. Securing the space for FanFest is a major part of any city's bid for the All-Star Game. Approximately two years before the All-Star Game, Secaira-Cotto leads a contingent of representatives from MLB and BaAM, the event's production company for the past 20 years, to the proposed FanFest site. Once the group arrives in the host city, it finalizes the location and begins the process of shaping the event to perfectly fit the convention hall's unique space. "Each city is very different," Secaira-Cotto said. "Each site has different shapes, different numbers of levels. We have to ask, 'How does our show fit into their space?'"

After the lease for the convention space is signed, Secaira-Cotto creates a timetable for the next two years. Work begins shortly thereafter, as the elements that will delight fans must be pieced together like a puzzle. The first logistical piece that needs to fall in place on the floorplan is the Aquafina Diamond, an 11,500-square-foot field that is always the largest element of the event. The diamond hosts anything from baseball clinics led by current Big Leaguers and Hall of Famers to a Home Run Derby featuring MLB team mascots. Once the diamond is situated, all other aspects of FanFest are placed around it. There are historical stops, such as the Cooperstown and Negro Leagues exhibits, a Hometown Heroes wing, which celebrates the host city's favorite sons, and a Collector's Showcase where fans can buy, sell and trade baseball collectibles and memorabilia.

There are also loads of interactive exhibits and games, from video batting cages to a Taco Bell–themed exhibit called "Steal a Base, Steal a Taco," in which fans race down a baseline and try to slide in safely before the play on the video screen ends, winning a taco for participating. There's a Sports Authority clubhouse store, encompassing some 6,000 square feet, where fans can purchase everything from a customized All-Star Game jersey to a collectible commemorative pin. There are also autograph tables scattered throughout, where legends will sign memorabilia for eager fans.

And no FanFest would be complete without the World's Largest Baseball. At 12 feet in diameter, the ball achieved *Guinness Book of World Records* status in 2006, and it's always among the first things fans see when they enter the show. Over the years, it has been signed by MLB legends such as Hank Aaron, Yogi Berra and Ted Williams, as well as by current stars like Derek Jeter and Torii Hunter. Fans can take photos in front of the ball, which is stored in its own trailer in a Toronto warehouse when not on display during All-Star Week.

As the All-Star Game draws near, the floorplan is approved in mid-May by local fire marshals, who, among other things, ensure that exhibits don't block exits and that walkways are wide enough to accommodate the huge crowds. MLB spends months working to design exhibits, collaborating with sponsors such as Scotts, the league's official lawn care company, to create something that will work well for the brand while also exciting fans. Secaira-Cotto's team traffics applications from exhibitors who are desperate for a piece of the action. "It's a huge fan event," Secaira-Cotto said. "There's nothing out there like it. Exhibitors realize that and come back year after year." MLB works to make sure that there's a balance of goods being sold — anything from Roberto Clemente buttons that went for $1 each in Pittsburgh to highly valuable, one-of-a-kind items.

Installation begins about 10 days before FanFest launches the All-Star festivities, which is also when Secaira-Cotto's team arrives on site. BaAM estimates that the event requires 10,000 hours of manpower, between installation, operation and disassembly, in addition to the help of 1,450 local volunteers who work at various booths and kiosks throughout the event's five days.

All of the preparation leads up to the Friday before the game, when two years of planning give way to a five-day All-Star party. Dignitaries such as mayors, governors, baseball officials and Hall of Famers often take part in the opening ceremony at FanFest, which features a formal ribbon-cutting that officially opens the event. From Friday through Tuesday, Secaira-Cotto's days often begin before 4:30 a.m. and end after a wrap-up production meeting that follows the close of each day at 8 p.m. most nights. During that time, she gives interviews to various morning news programs, leads VIPs around the exhibits and shuttles between her on-site office and the floor to troubleshoot any problems that arise. "You're running on adrenaline," she said. "You just want to make it bigger and better than previous years."

FANDEMONIUM
The Baseball Hall of Fame exhibit is always a hit at All-Star FanFest.

UNCONVENTIONAL
Each year, the host city's
convention center turns into a
must-see baseball wonderland.

MAKING HISTORY
The All-Star Gala was held at the American Museum of Natural History in New York City in 2008.

GALA

IF ALL-STAR WEEK IS ONE BIG PARTY, THEN THE OFFICIAL MLB ALL-Star Gala is its *piece de resistance.* The event welcomes 5,000 invited guests each year and celebrates the All-Stars, the host city and the Midsummer Classic. Featuring exciting musical acts and entertainers, along with delicious food, often from local establishments, the Gala is a highlight of the week.

MLB looks to host the party in a unique setting every year, from the Grove in Anaheim in 2010 to the American Museum of Natural History in New York for the 2008 game to a pier in the shadow of the Bay Bridge for the 2007 event in San Francisco. Part of what made the Grove so convenient was that it shares a parking lot with Angel Stadium, a great benefit for fans heading over to the Gala from the ballpark after the Home Run Derby.

Recent galas have included performances from musical acts such as pop singer Colbie Caillat, rapper Nelly and R&B star Macy Gray. The event also gives guests the chance to rub elbows with Dustin Pedroia or Hall of Famer Hank Aaron.

Originally organized by the host teams at upscale venues such as the Pfister Hotel in Milwaukee in 1975, Philadelphia's Independence Mall Theatre in '76 and Kiana Island just outside of Seattle in '79, MLB assumed control of the Gala and other All-Star hospitality events during the mid-1980s under the direction of Commissioner Peter Ueberroth. Since then, production of the Gala has been coordinated with local event companies, which help MLB plan the festivities once the location is secured. Eileen Buser, MLB's senior director of special events, sends out requests for proposals to local vendors, seeking to work with companies familiar to the host team. The proposals that are returned don't include a full creative plan for the event, but they do give MLB a taste of potential themes for the party. "One of the main priorities of the parties is to make them feel local," Buser said. "We want them to feel unique to the host city." That meant a cowboy theme in Houston in 2004, a Motor City schematic in Detroit for the 2005 party and SoCal style in 2010.

Entertainers perform hour-long sets at the Gala, and they're the main draws of the evening, with local talent taking the stage first. In addition to the marquee acts, guests are entertained by constant live music and various performers around the venue. And on the way out, guests are given a party favor to remember the night — sometimes an official All-Star Game baseball or, in Anaheim, a miniature Mickey Mouse statue decorated with MLB team logos, replicas of the giant statues found throughout Southern California prior to the game.

In Anaheim in 2010, MLB booked the entertainment and coordinated the catering, while Buser's team chose Silver Birches, an event design company, to handle the creative aspects. The operation involves having nearly 300 chefs on site to ensure that all food stations and pass-around servers are stocked. Buser works throughout the night, handling any issues that come up, from identifying which buffet tables and bars are getting the most traffic to ensuring the safe and comfortable dispersing of crowds. There's always one person from the event company shadowing her, helping to quickly resolve any problems. The hope every year is to create a memorable and exciting night, one that guests remember as a highlight of All-Star Week.

TAILGATE PARTY

ONCE THE GALA IS OVER, ATTENTION SHIFTS IMMEDIATELY to the next party. And, as with everything else during the controlled chaos of All-Star Week, it has to happen very, very quickly. The Official All-Star Pregame Party — billed as a family-friendly tailgate, a far more casual affair than the Gala — takes place on the day of the Midsummer Classic. As was the case in Anaheim in 2010, it's often held in the same location as the Gala, which ends about 16 hours before the Pregame Party begins. Despite the shared space, the two events are treated separately during the planning phase.

"They're night and day," said Eileen Buser, MLB's senior director of special events. MLB's goal is to create two distinct events that nonetheless can transition seamlessly and quickly. In Anaheim, that meant erecting a ferris wheel and skateboarding halfpipe overnight, while covering all of the surfaces from the previous night's Gala in white, offering a more casual vibe. Train, the band that performed on-field before the previous night's Home Run Derby, played a set during the party.

There are unique challenges to hosting two parties in a single space. "You try to keep as many things consistent between the parties, but find ways to make them look different," Buser said. "The elements for Tuesday are all loaded in before the Gala. They just have to be creatively covered by something on Monday night."

Sometimes, as in 2010, MLB works with a single event company for the two different parties. But in other years, as in Detroit in 2005, two different companies take part. No matter what happens behind the scenes, many local suppliers are ultimately involved, and the Pregame Party remains a fun and distinct event.

PREGAME SHOWCASE

THE BASEBALL TALENT ON HAND DURING ALL-STAR WEEK CAN be overwhelming at times. But with a massive TV audience and fans in the ballpark waiting for a show, Major League Baseball uses the All-Star pregame ceremony to up the wow factor even higher. Whether starring a cast member from a hit TV program like *Glee*, the best hitter who ever lived or even the president of the United States, MLB always opens the Midsummer Classic broadcast with a flourish.

"The pregame ceremony says something about who we are as Major League Baseball," said Brian O'Gara, MLB's senior director of special events, who serves as the on-field director during the All-Star Game. "We use it as a showcase." In recent years, that showcase has seen MLB honor all living Hall of Famers before the 2008 contest, Hall of Famer Willie Mays in 2007, and, in 2009 and '10, the 30 "All-Stars Among Us," everyday heroes from MLB communities.

Planning begins in early spring, when officials at MLB, under the direction of Executive Vice President, Business, Tim Brosnan, begin determining what they want to do with their blank canvas. Over the course of the next few months, they will determine how to stage all of the elements of the ceremony, how to integrate the themes with the players, and how to engage the fans watching at home and those in the stadium at the same time. In 2009 and 2010, MLB believed that the times called for a message of community outreach and support amid the country's severe economic woes.

For the "All-Stars Among Us" ceremony in 2010, that message was achieved through a video of celebrities addressing the need for community volunteers. MLB Chief Marketing Officer Jacqueline Parkes often reaches out to these stars, requesting their participation through relationships with the charitable group Stand Up 2 Cancer and the Entertainment Industry Foundation. Ben Affleck, Sheryl Crow, Harrison Ford and Julia Roberts were among the A-list stars who participated in the video, which told the stories of many of the 30 community All-Stars who were honored on-field. The faces were different, but the message was similar to the 2009 ceremony at Busch Stadium, when all five living U.S. presidents spoke about community service and the "All-Stars Among Us" in a video that aligned with MLB's marketing slogan, "Go Beyond." That year, the culmination of the pregame festivities was a ceremonial first pitch thrown by President Barack Obama.

Rehearsals for the opening ceremony begin five days before the All-Star Game, with volunteers standing in for players and celebrities. The ceremony evolves somewhat during rehearsals, accounting for timing issues and other, less predictable concerns. One such case arose in 2008, when there was a small problem during rehearsal for the Hall

EASY RIDER
Hall of Famer Willie Mays was given a
warm welcome at AT&T Park in 2007.

of Famers' entrance. The plan had been for the All-Star reserves to assemble along the baselines, after which the Hall of Famers in attendance would assume their former positions on the diamond. They were to be joined by the '08 All-Star starters, who would run out to their positions after being introduced. But placing the reserves on the lines created a sightline problem, blocking the array of Hall of Famers and making it difficult to appreciate the moment. After noticing it during rehearsal, the reserves were moved to the basepaths, giving everyone in the stadium a better view.

Usually, though, the practices are about familiarizing participants with the ceremony and creating a time sheet that's cued to the second. For the sake of the broadcast, and because there are often planes en route to the park for a flyover, it's important that from the moment the ceremony begins until the end of the national anthem, everything is timed carefully. MLB and Fox staffers come armed with stopwatches during rehearsal to ensure that it goes according to schedule.

Once the ceremony begins, though, you just have to hope that everything goes as planned. "You only have one chance to get it right," O'Gara said. "During the regular season, with 81 home games a year, you can fix something the next day. But for the All-Star Game

> *For the sake of the broadcast, and because there are often planes en route to the park for a flyover, it's important that from the moment the ceremony begins until the end of the anthem, everything is timed carefully.*

we have 364 days to grit our teeth over any mistakes." O'Gara is usually in the press box with the Fox stage manager and the stadium scoreboard operator during the ceremony, giving directions into a headset. It's a great spot to oversee all that is happening on the field, but it's too far away to communicate — even nonverbally — with anyone not plugged into his microphone. Over the years, though, as he has gotten to know players by working with them in one Midsummer Classic after another, he has come to lean on certain guys to help him when it's go-time.

"Derek Jeter is like an extra stage manager," he said. "We'll tell him: 'This is what we're doing, this is when we need players to start moving. If you do it, everyone will follow.' He understands the impact and importance of what we are doing and is very supportive." The strategy has paid off time and again. In 2007, when Willie Mays was brought onto the field in San Francisco and surrounded by the All-Stars, it was Jeter who made the first move toward the legendary center fielder, with everyone else following. And in 2010, with the All-Stars on the foul lines and the "All-Stars Among Us" on the infield grass, Jeter was the first player to head toward the community heroes, with everyone falling in line behind him once again.

FIRST TOSS President Barack Obama showcased his southpaw skills during the 2009 All-Star pregame ceremony at Busch Stadium.

ALL-CENTURY TEAM

MORE THAN 13,000 PLAYERS TOOK THE FIELD DURING THE 20th century. At the 1999 All-Star Game, Major League Baseball celebrated 100 of those it deemed the best of the best — the nominees for its All-Century Team — for one night.

Each living member of the esteemed group was invited to the pregame ceremony, and 32 ultimately lined the field at Boston's Fenway Park, the quintessential host, nearly a century old itself — it opened in 1912 — and certainly steeped in tradition.

"Last game of the century. Boston. Fenway Park. A lot of nostalgia," AL Manager Joe Torre said.

MLB's legends stepped onto the field from an opening in the center-field wall and made their way across the outfield grass toward the infield diamond. As the All-Century nominees were introduced, modern-day honorees like Ken Griffey Jr., Randy Johnson and Cal Ripken Jr. found themselves shoulder-to-shoulder with heroes of yesteryear such as Willie Mays, Bob Gibson, Stan Musial and Warren Spahn, among others.

The climax came with the dramatic entrance of legendary Red Sox slugger Ted Williams. The 80-year-old rode in on a golf cart decorated with his familiar No. 9. He waved to fans as the cart motored down the right-field line toward the mound. Despite having suffered a broken hip and two strokes in recent years, Williams rose from the cart and threw the ceremonial first pitch to former Red Sox catcher Carlton Fisk before more than 34,000 fans who had packed into Fenway for the Classic.

"Wasn't it great!" Williams said of the emotional welcome he received. "I can only describe it as great. It didn't surprise me all that much because I know how these fans are here in Boston. They love this game as much as any players, and Boston's lucky to have the faithful Red Sox fans. They're the best."

All of the current and former Big League legends on the field at Fenway quickly converged upon Boston's "Splendid Splinter" in an emotional gesture that bridged several generations of baseball's top talents. For his part, Williams was just as eager to speak with the top hitters of the present day such as Tony Gwynn, Sammy Sosa and Larry Walker.

Red Sox ace Pedro Martinez was honored as an All-Star that year and was thrilled to be in the presence of such legends. "Representing the decade, the last one of the century," he said, "being there with all those players around us — I never, never expected it."

'THE MAN' AMONG BOYS All-Stars like Mark McGwire (left) were awestruck by legends like Stan Musial at the 1999 Midsummer Classic.

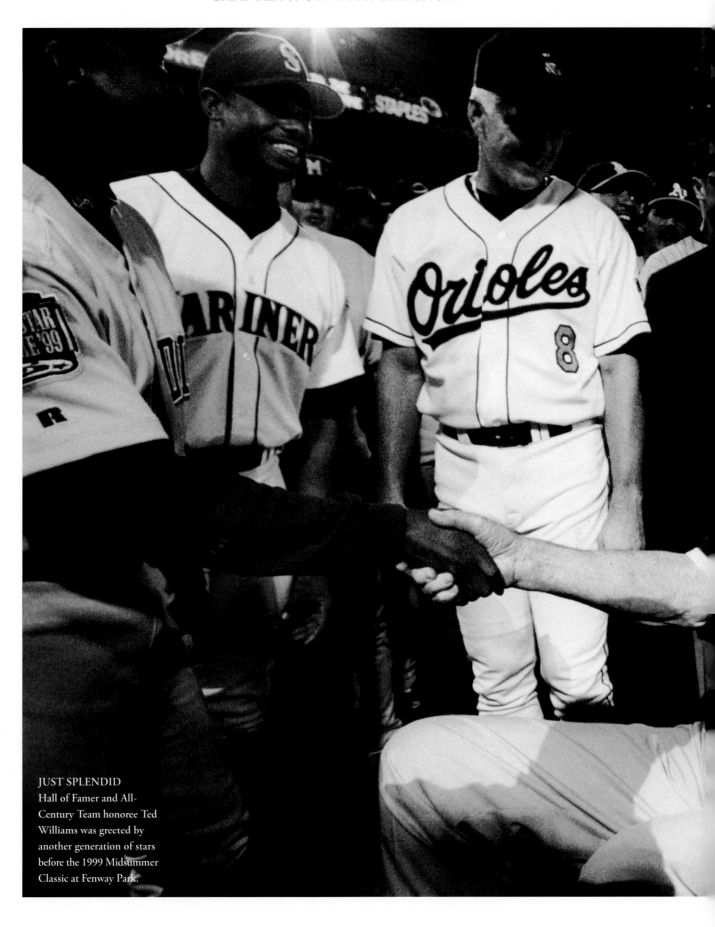

JUST SPLENDID
Hall of Famer and All-Century Team honoree Ted Williams was greeted by another generation of stars before the 1999 Midsummer Classic at Fenway Park.

POMP AND CIRCUMSTANCE

Of course, a major part of the pregame ceremony every year is the singing of the "Star-Spangled Banner," with MLB and Fox seeking musical stars to excite the fans in-stadium and at home. In 2010, Amber Riley, from the hit Fox show *Glee*, sang the anthem at Angel Stadium while standing on a special circular stage constructed over the mound and surrounded by members of both All-Star teams, as well as the 30 "All-Stars Among Us" honored by *People* magazine and MLB.

Unlike the World Series, for which the location is not set until just days before the games are played and which features separate national anthems on up to seven different dates, the All-Star Game performance is a once-a-year honor that attracts some of the biggest names in the business. From Carrie Underwood in 2006 to Chris Isaak in 2007 to Sheryl Crow in 2009, it's a distinguished group that has serenaded fans with the song on the Midsummer Classic field.

The act follows the performance of the Canadian national anthem. In recent years, the "Star-Spangled Banner" has been accompanied by the unfurling of a massive flag in center field. And, when possible, the anthem is followed by a U.S. military flyover — a challenging logistical maneuver that creates an awesome effect. During the ceremony, the planes are holding in the air, waiting for a "Go" call from MLB and Fox, which usually comes right before the network cuts to commercial. With the timing set during rehearsals, the pilots know exactly when they are supposed to get in position, and, unless the singer unexpectedly milks the moment or holds a note too long, the flyover should occur right on time, as the anthem ends.

The national anthems aren't the only patriotic songs performed during the All-Star Game. During the seventh-inning stretch, MLB brings out another star — Josh Groban in 2008, Sara Evans in '09 and Colbie Caillat in 2010 — to sing "God Bless America," a performance also broadcast live on Fox.

READY, JET, GO! Military planes flew over U.S. Cellular Field before the 2003 All-Star Game.

STARS AND PIPES
Missouri-native Sheryl Crow sang the national anthem at the 2009 All-Star Game in St. Louis.

ROLL CALL

For many All-Stars, the experience doesn't quite feel real until they hear their names announced over the stadium's public address system during pregame introductions. It's at that moment, as they line up with their fellow honorees, when it really hits home that they're being recognized among the elite.

These days, Fox airs the introductions live, with Joe Buck's voice resonating through the stadium PA system as well as in the homes of fans around the world. The reserves take the field together and are introduced down the line — first the visitors, then the home league. The starters from each league are then called individually from the dugout. The moment is fraught with emotion, and the All-Star Game's light and joyful mood offers little protection for rivals in town for the festivities, as home fans always give their foes some grief. In New York in 2008, the boos for Red Sox players were, if not as intense as you would hear during the regular season, then pretty close. But the players have learned to laugh it off.

Local boys, however, always get to enjoy the experience the most. "I remember in Pittsburgh, Freddy Sanchez got called out and the fans went crazy," Barry Zito said about the 2006 All-Star Game. "They were like, 'Pittsburgh's own Freddy Sanchez,' and I was like, 'Man, that is so cool.'"

THE VOICE OF GOD

For decades, a part of the majesty of Yankee Stadium was the stentorian voice of public address announcer Bob Sheppard. Born in Queens, N.Y., in 1910, Sheppard's precise diction and inimitable baritone made him the voice of New York sports for generations of fans. After getting his start with the Brooklyn Dodgers, Sheppard made his Yankee Stadium debut in 1951. He would be a Bronx staple until his death in July 2010. Reggie Jackson famously declared him the "Voice of God."

When Sheppard passed away at age 99, just days before the 2010 Midsummer Classic, Brian O'Gara, MLB's senior director of special events, came up with a touching tribute. He obtained a recording of Sheppard introducing Derek Jeter that had been used during the 2008 All-Star Game. O'Gara warned Jeter that the introduction when he came to the plate for his first at-bat would be a bit longer than normal. Jeter took his time, working on his bat in the on-deck circle instead of going right to the batter's box, as Sheppard's voice said: "Now batting, for the American League, from the New York Yankees, the shortstop, No. 2, Derek Jeter, No. 2."

"I didn't want him to be standing in the batter's box while it was happening — which could appear awkward and uncomfortable," said O'Gara. "That's why you rehearse, to anticipate every detail."

FIRE STARTERS
Taking the field during introductions is a thrill for All-Stars, like Bobby Abreu in 2005.

PRESIDENTS

SINCE BASEBALL HAS LONG BEEN KNOWN AS THE NATIONAL pastime, it only makes sense that the nation's commander in chief would have the honor of throwing out the ceremonial first pitch. That was precisely the case in 2009, when President Barack Obama took the hill at Busch Stadium in St. Louis to get the 80th All-Star Game underway. Showing pride for his hometown team, the 44th president emerged from the National League dugout clad in a White Sox jacket. After conferring with a flock of Cardinals legends on the field, the left-handed Obama strode to the top of the mound, toed the rubber and fired home.

"Given the economic turmoil the country was going through at the time and the historic nature of his presidency, President Obama throwing the first pitch to Albert Pujols in St. Louis in 2009 was a major highlight in the history of the All-Star Game," said Tim Brosnan, Major League Baseball's executive vice president of business.

Although the security concerns involved in having the sitting president throw out the first pitch are extensive, there is no doubting the impact. Before President Obama took the mound at Busch Stadium to open the All-Star Game, he was joined by all five living U.S. presidents in a seven-minute video to pay tribute to the remarkable citizens honored by MLB and *People* magazine as part of the "All-Stars Among Us" initiative. The video salute represented an unprecedented collaboration between Presidents Obama, George W. Bush, Bill Clinton, George H.W. Bush and Jimmy Carter. The moment, encouraging fans across the country to make community service a priority in their lives, marked the first time that all of the living presidents participated in any sporting event.

"No major sport had ever taken its biggest marketing platform and dedicated it to 30 people in local communities across the United States," said Brosnan. "Not only were we the first, but we did it with the full participation of the president of the United States."

President Obama was the sixth sitting U.S. president to throw out the ceremonial first pitch at the All-Star Game, following in the footsteps of George H.W. Bush, Gerald Ford, Richard M. Nixon, John F. Kennedy and Franklin Delano Roosevelt.

"Having a president involved really elevates the entire pre-game ceremony. It's a moment that manages to be special for both the fans in the ballpark and those watching at home," said Marla Miller, MLB's senior vice president of special events.

In 1937, FDR rode out onto the field at Griffith Stadium in Washington, D.C., in an open car in front of 31,391 fans. Before starters Dizzy Dean and Lefty Gomez opened the fourth installment of the Midsummer Classic, Roosevelt tossed the ball into play from his first-row seat.

A generation later, President Kennedy and Vice President Lyndon B. Johnson attended the 1962 Midsummer Classic, with JFK tossing a pitch from his seat in the stands. Kennedy also shared a historic moment with one of the game's all-time greats. Kennedy called over Cardinals star Stan Musial to congratulate him on a sixth-inning pinch-hit and famously proffered a few words of encouragement for the Hall of Famer, who was in the twilight of his career.

"A couple years ago they told me I was too young to be president and you were too old to be playing baseball. But we fooled them," Kennedy said.

The history of presidential pitches gained another chapter when Nixon tossed two — one to American League catcher Bill Freehan and one to NL catcher Johnny Bench — before the 1970 All-Star Game at Riverfront Stadium in Cincinnati. Luckily, neither of the starting backstops was behind the plate when Pete Rose came barreling down the third-base line looking to score the final run of the game. Back-up AL backstop Ray Fosse bore the brunt of that blow and was severely injured for his trouble.

Bench added to his own personal All-Star scrapbook in 1976 when he again found himself part of a presidential battery. Ford, who had been a key member of two national championship football teams at the University of Michigan, threw right-handed to Bench and then left-handed to Carlton Fisk to open the 1976 Midsummer Classic at Veterans Stadium in Philadelphia in the summer of America's bicentennial.

The elder Bush would be the last president to toss out the first pitch at an All-Star Game — he did so at San Diego's Jack Murphy Stadium in 1992 — until Obama's 2009 toss to Pujols in St. Louis. After leaving the field, Obama joined Fox broadcasters in the booth during the game.

"This is the national pastime," Obama said during his visit to the booth. "To go down there and meet Stan Musial and Bob Gibson and those guys, it's such a reminder about what's great in this country. You can't beat that and it's a real treat."

President Ford, a key member of two national championship football teams at the University of Michigan, threw right-handed to Johnny Bench and left-handed to Carlton Fisk to open the 1976 Midsummer Classic at Veterans Stadium in Philadelphia in the summer of America's bicentennial.

SIT 'EM DOWN
President Richard M. Nixon kicked off the 1970 All-Star Game at Riverfront Stadium in Cincinnati by tossing the ball from his front-row seat.

CHAPTER 7:
TUESDAY

AFTER YEARS OF PLANNING, WEEKS OF FINE-TUNING AND A MEMORABLE FEW days of revelry, the game everyone in baseball has been waiting for has arrived. As enjoyable as the ancillary events have been, it's impossible to deny that Tuesday is the focus of All-Star Week. No one knows what will transpire until the All-Stars assemble between the lines, displaying a strange but brilliant array of uniforms. It might be a contest like the one in 2010, when the NL avenged more than a decade of defeats. The story in 2003 was 22-year-old Hank Blalock drilling a two-run home run late in the game to give the Junior Circuit home-field advantage in October. Regardless of the result, some hometown heroes are sure to dazzle, and some hyped youngsters will take the field next to seasoned stars. There may be touching moments and tightly contested duels. But whatever happens, the joining of each league's All-Star forces — now with more than just pride on the line — will make for a game unlike any other. And in the end, one league's triumph will earn bragging rights. At least until next year.

IMPRESSIVE LINEUP Once the players are on the lines — as the AL was here in 2009 — All-Star Game action is imminent.

THE MAIN EVENT

AND FINALLY, ON TUESDAY, THE BEST BASEBALL PLAYERS IN THE WORLD get to do what they all came together for in the first place.

Make no mistake, the pageantry of All-Star Week, from the parties to the parades, is a real part of its appeal, and it's hard to envision the event doing anything but expanding in years to come. Nevertheless, when the All-Stars assemble on the first- and third-base lines each year for the national anthem, there's no doubt that the main event is about to begin.

Since Babe Ruth hit the first All-Star Game home run in 1933, the Midsummer Classic has been one of the most entertaining contests on baseball's calendar, even if it is remembered more for individual moments than for final game results. It's about stirring instances like Cal Ripken Jr. getting pushed toward shortstop by Alex Rodriguez before going deep in his final All-Star appearance, or Dwight Gooden pitching in the game as a 19-year-old, or Fred Lynn hitting the first grand slam in the event's history at the 1983 game in Chicago, or Jackie Robinson stepping onto the field in 1949 and finally integrating the All-Star Game.

By collecting each league's best players, the event has always brought together strange bedfellows. Now that the game's outcome determines Fall Classic home-field advantage, you're more likely than ever to see Red Sox fans cheering on guys like Derek Jeter or Brewers players celebrating their own division rivals. "For me, Albert Pujols is that guy," said Milwaukee's Ryan Braun. "He's the guy that I really enjoy watching play. He's — in my opinion — the best player in baseball, and it's fun to get an opportunity to watch him go about his business for a couple of days and to see how he conducts himself, figure out his routine and see what helps make him successful."

Even with the high stakes, camaraderie and lighthearted moments are the norm during the Classic. With many players donning microphones for the television broadcast, fans really get to see and hear how much fun they're having. And sometimes, as in 2002, the difference in approach is visible. The year after he set the single-season home run record, Barry Bonds came into Milwaukee for the All-Star Game as the sport's most feared slugger and immediately showed why when he crushed a Derek Lowe pitch to center field. Torii Hunter, then with the Twins, raced back and leapt at the wall to make an incredible catch, robbing Bonds of a home run and ending the inning. (Coincidentally, the wall, at almost the exact spot where Hunter made the catch, had an image of a fully extended player catching a ball.) As a beaming Hunter left the field and the broadcast got ready to cut to commercial, a laughing Bonds ran over to him and picked Hunter up over his shoulder in mock anger. It was a jovial and fun moment, and Bonds followed it up in proper form — by hitting a homer in his next at-bat.

Of all the memorable superstar interactions in All-Star history, it's hard to beat the trio lining up in the NL outfield during the 1960s. For 23 innings across three Midsummer Classics, the Senior Circuit was able to

STAR-SPANGLED EVENING
After the leagues have been announced,
the national anthem sung and the
American flag unfurled, the All-Star
Game is ready to begin.

showcase Hank Aaron in left, Willie Mays in center and Roberto Clemente in right. Hall of Famer Tom Seaver recalled entering the game as a reliever in 1967 and looking out to check his fielders' positioning. "I stopped cold," Seaver said. "The moment almost overwhelmed me. I had never experienced anything like this. Aaron, Mays, Clemente — all there at once behind me. Was this real?"

It was real. But it generally happens just once a year — although there were two All-Star Games from 1959–62 to boost the players' pension fund. Once you get past the strange collection of jerseys sharing the field, the All-Star Game is the most natural part of the week. It plays out like a regular game, even if there are more pitching changes and fewer strategic managerial moves. There are blowouts and nail biters, games called due to rain and 15-inning thrillers. More than anything, though, there are the best hitters against the best pitchers.

And even now, nearly eight decades after the first showcase, fans still get to witness new things. The 2008 game was the longest by time — four hours and 50 minutes — in history. And the 2007 matchup saw Ichiro Suzuki hit the first Midsummer Classic inside-the-park home run — and send MLB's PR team scrambling. Along with his unconventional roundtripper, which ricocheted bizarrely off the bricks in the San Francisco outfield, Ichiro had a 3-for-3 day. But once he left the game, he was planning on heading home — like some players do — to enjoy a day off before the second half. Problem was that Ichiro was a pretty good bet to be named the game's MVP; but with a tight game, anything could happen in the late innings. Realizing that they wanted Ichiro to stick around but without wanting

HOMEWARD BOUND

Before either league had anything other than pride at stake in the All-Star Game, one play stood out as the contest's most famous, fueling debates about competition and sportsmanship in an exhibition.

Heading into the 1970 contest at Cincinnati's Riverfront Stadium, the NL carried a seven-year winning streak. But the AL threatened to break it, keeping the game tied in extra innings.

Finally, in the bottom of the 12th, NL star Pete Rose singled, then advanced to second on a base hit. What happened next has entered history. Rose took off on a single to center, rounded third and barreled down on Indians catcher Ray Fosse as the throw came in. The ball arrived just before him, but Rose lowered his shoulder and slammed into Fosse with such force that not only the ball, but also Fosse's glove, were knocked loose as Rose crossed home with the winning run. Rose insisted that he collided with Fosse to avoid a late slide that could have caused serious injury, but Fosse wasn't so sure. "Maybe he should have run around me. It all happened so quick. I never got hit like that before."

to definitively state the reason, members of MLB's PR group tracked him down before he could leave and encouraged him to stay. In the end, Ichiro accepted the Ted Williams MVP Award — and a Chevy Tahoe Hybrid — on the field after the AL won, 5-4.

FRIENDLY SHOVE
Alex Rodriguez (left) surrendered his spot at short to Cal Ripken Jr. in 2001, Ripken's final All-Star Game.

STREAKING

THE ALL-STAR GAME IS BASEBALL'S MIDSUMMER CONSTANT. THE WINNING LEAGUE IS ANYTHING but. That is, however, except for a few dominant runs.

Before its 2010 victory at Angel Stadium, the National League's last All-Star triumph came in Philadelphia in 1996, when Dodgers catcher Mike Piazza sparked a 6-0 win and took the game's MVP Award. For a record 13 years following that game, the American League managed not to lose a single contest to its rival circuit.

"You wouldn't think it would be that lopsided," said three-time All-Star Andy Pettitte in 2010. "The National League has a great team, great players, great pitchers. I know the last few have been extremely close."

The lone year the AL didn't register a win during the streak came in 2002 at Milwaukee's Miller Park, when both teams ran out of pitchers in the 11th inning and the game ended in a 7-7 tie.

"I think that if you did this for the next 300 years, you probably wouldn't see one team win 12 in a row," said 2010 All-Star Game MVP Brian McCann, an NL representative. "I think it's just one of those freak things that happened."

Some observers theorize that the heated competition to sign star free-agent players between the Yankees and Red Sox has raised the bar for the rest of the American League. Others credit the AL's superiority coming about as a result of the designated hitter rule, the presence of progressive front offices and some recent lopsided interleague trades.

But AL dominance wasn't always the case. From 1963–82, the NL won 19 of 20 All-Star Games. It boasted win streaks of eight and 11 games, respectively, interrupted only by the 1971 matchup, when Oakland's Reggie Jackson homered off a transformer atop Tiger Stadium's roof to lead the Junior Circuit to a 6-4 victory. Between 1950 and '87, AL All-Stars won just eight Midsummer Classics, tying one other. The stretch was particularly devastating considering that the AL had taken 12 of the first 16 All-Star Games.

ALL-STAR CATHEDRAL

There's nothing like an All-Star Game at Yankee Stadium. Four were held there — a distinction shared only by Cleveland Municipal Stadium, the Indians' home from 1932–93. The Bronx first hosted the Midsummer Classic, the marquee event of that year's New York World's Fair, in 1939. Ten Yankees players — including Lou Gehrig — were in uniform, and the crowd got a preview of Game 1 of the '39 World Series when the Yanks' Red Ruffing faced the Reds' Paul Derringer, as the AL was victorious, 3-1.

Another Midsummer Classic, memorable as slugger Ted Williams' final All-Star appearance, came to town in 1960. Unfortunately for the AL hosts, the park became the NL's grandstand; Stan Musial blasted a homer into the right-field upper deck for his sixth All-Star longball, a record that still stands.

The NL prevailed at Yankee Stadium again in 1977. Baltimore ace Jim Palmer's scoreless-innings streak couldn't outlast his mark of eight, and instead Senior Circuit starting pitcher Don Sutton threw three of his own blank frames to take the game's MVP Award.

When the contest returned to the Big Apple in 2008, the final season in old Yankee Stadium, the AL made it count. In a 15-inning, four-hour and 50-minute duel — the longest Midsummer Classic ever by time — the AL extended its unbeaten streak to a record 13 games on a J.D. Drew homer and game-winning sacrifice fly by Michael Young in the 15th.

"It seemed like the Stadium didn't want it to end," said Derek Jeter, one of three Yankees representing the AL in '08. "I thought it was fitting."

HEROES WELCOME
The red carpet ushered All-Stars toward San Francisco's AT&T Park for the 2007 game.

MAGIC CARPET RIDE

As any paparazzo worth his weight in lens cleaner will attest, there is no spectacle quite like a Hollywood awards show. Million-watt smiles light up the night as everyone who is anyone in the movie industry parades past thousands of fans and flashbulbs. The pageantry of those events gave Tim Brosnan, MLB's executive vice president, business, an idea: If Hollywood could showcase its biggest stars on a red carpet, why couldn't baseball?

The framework was already in place. For decades, baseball's best have gathered for the All-Star Game. But until recently, the players arrived in buses with blacked-out windows on roads blocked to the public. That all changed with the first All-Star Game *Red Carpet Show* in Detroit in 2005, which gave Big Leaguers a chance to be treated like Tinseltown royalty. Players boarded classic Chevrolet convertibles for the '05 red carpet run to Comerica Park on Woodward Avenue.

"Fans love the *Red Carpet Show*," Brosnan said. "It has become an integral piece of the week's celebration. Taking over the All-Star city's downtown area and parading the best players the game has to offer in front of hundreds of thousands of fans has turned the *Red Carpet Show* into one of the annual highlights of All-Star."

In 2006, more than 40,000 fans in Pittsburgh lined the picturesque Roberto Clemente Bridge and the streets leading up to PNC Park to welcome the All-Stars. Players arrived in new fuel-efficient trucks provided by local Chevrolet dealers, many of whom drove the cars during the procession. Entertainment celebrities have also attended the festivities, with some even serving as player chauffeurs. Since 2009, MLB Network has filmed each All-Star along the route.

With MLB staffers ushering the players into their vehicles, the event is carried out with exacting precision. The 2008 red carpet in New York City was the longest ever and extended up Sixth Avenue into Central Park. In 2010, the parade didn't end at the ballpark, as is customary, either; instead it went to nearby Disneyland for a one-of-a-kind event. For the players, a major publicity appearance is rarely part of their pregame routine, but having time to mingle in the green room before the *Red Carpet Show* makes for a fun, even relaxing, afternoon.

"It was pretty cool," said Michael Young, MVP of the 2006 game. "It really has turned into a great event. The fans are very enthusiastic, and there's just a lot of energy. I think, of the four big sports, Major League Baseball does the best job with its All-Star Game."

BACKSEAT DRIVER All-Star Ichiro Suzuki made his way to PNC Park in '06.

ONCE UPON A DREAM The 2010 red carpet parade through Anaheim ended in Disneyland.

PAPI ON PARADE
David Ortiz took a red carpet ride
before the 2005 Midsummer Classic.

LEADING MEN

On most days of the season, any Major League manager would love to face the "dilemma" of choosing between Ryan Howard, Adrian Gonzalez and Albert Pujols to start at first base. Such was the puzzle confronting Phillies skipper Charlie Manuel when he helmed the National League squad in the 2010 All-Star Game. He spent most of his flight from Philadelphia to Anaheim working out his lineup. Ultimately, Pujols started at first, having won the fan vote; Howard was the starting DH; and Gonzalez entered the game as a substitute.

"The lineup is probably the toughest thing to make out," Yankees skipper Joe Girardi said in 2010, when he had the honor of managing the AL All-Star team. "We spend time talking about it. There were changes — there were additions, subtractions — and it's the hardest thing."

Although they may be burdened with an embarrassment of riches, All-Star managers — skippers from the previous year's pennant winning teams — don't have as simple a job at it may seem. Not only do they have to balance the expectations of each player on their roster and the various concerns of the clubs from whom those players are on loan, but home-field advantage for the upcoming World Series has been at stake since 2003. That's quite a lot to juggle during a long weekend that is billed as a "break."

"When I managed in the All-Star Game before, I didn't really have much of that," Tigers Manager Jim Leyland said in 2007 as he recalled taking the reins in the Midsummer Classic before the stakes were raised. "I let the players do their thing. The game was more of a show then. It's different now, with the situation of home-field advantage in the World Series."

Regardless of how badly a skipper wants to win the game, though, it's difficult to be an aggressive manager. Putting aside the celebratory atmosphere of All-Star Week and the desire to get every player a moment in the spotlight, the players and coaches just don't have the time to prepare and implement the complex signs that take countless hours for a club to fine tune each year during Spring Training. Despite the high talent level on the field for the Midsummer Classic, there's no substitute for the familiarity and timing that players develop over the course of the season on their own teams — which is why weapons like the stolen base and the sacrifice are not always utilized in All-Star play. In 2006, NL skipper Phil Garner informed players that he would call for a bunt simply by pantomiming the motion in the dugout. Not exactly the most covert way to make a strategic move, but perhaps the best means of getting the message across given the circumstances.

"If it was just an exhibition game, I think, as a manager, you're going to try and get everybody involved, if possible," Tampa Bay Rays Manager Joe Maddon said in 2009. "The fact that the game has implications attached to it, then you're going to have to work this game entirely different. [It means] sitting down in advance, looking at how you're specifically going to use the pitchers, as much as anything. Regarding the position players, you should have enough by the end of the game."

LEADERS OF THE PACK
Managers Tony La Russa and Lou Piniella helmed the AL and NL, respectively, for the 1991 contest.

COMIC RELIEF

WITH THE MOST TALENTED BALLPLAYERS IN THE GAME FACING OFF IN FRONT OF A RAUCOUS packed house and a national TV audience — not to mention the home-field advantage in the World Series that has been hanging in the balance since 2003 — one might expect the All-Star Game to be a nervy affair. Fresh-faced first-timers may feel like they're in over their heads sharing a dugout with players who they idolized growing up, while wizened veterans may be wary of ceding the spotlight to those same ascending hot shots.

But Mariners All-Star staple Ichiro Suzuki has been bringing levity to the game since his debut in 2001. For years, the worst kept secret in the American League has been the Japanese superstar's annual comedic, profanity-laced pep talk about beating the National League just before the players charge onto the field each July. Not only does Ichiro, who generally communicates with the media through a translator, manage to get his teammates fired up before the top of the first inning, but he also diffuses any tension by getting everyone to share a laugh.

"If you've never seen it, it's definitely something pretty funny," Twins first baseman and four-time AL All-Star Justin Morneau told *Yahoo!* in 2010. "It's hard to explain the effect it has on everyone. It's such a tense environment. Everyone's a little nervous for the game, and then he comes out. He doesn't say a whole lot the whole time he's in there, and all of a sudden, the manager gets done with his speech, and he pops off."

Although it's back to business once the game is underway, there have been a handful of lighthearted moments that occurred on the field over the years, too. And just like any slapstick comedy, laughs often come at someone's expense. Few players in All-Star Game history have found themselves in the hot water that Phillies first baseman John Kruk did during the 1993 Midsummer Classic.

Kruk was a fine left-handed hitter for many years, but with a career average against southpaws that was 43 points lower than his average against righties, he would hardly have been the choice to hit against a tough left-handed hurler in a big spot. Finding himself in such a situation during the '93 All-Star Game, he must have been nervous as he strode to the batter's box to face perhaps the most intimidating southpaw of all time: Seattle's Randy Johnson, owner of a triple-digit fastball that he was still learning to harness. As Kruk dug in at the plate to face Johnson for the first time in his career, the Big Unit unleashed his first pitch, but it got away, sailing over and behind the terrified Kruk's head. Like someone who had just narrowly averted a traffic accident, the dazed Kruk needed a moment to collect his wits before heading back into the batter's box — this time standing about a foot further from the plate.

Kruk flailed meekly at the next three pitches, all low and away, and seemed relieved just to head back to the visitor's dugout with only his dignity injured. "The ball just got away," Johnson said of the first pitch, "but John has the type of personality that he didn't think anything of it." The next batter, Cincinnati's Barry Larkin, recalled his view from the on-deck circle: "I laughed. Then I thought, 'Oh Lord, I've got to get up there next.'"

Although Kruk's close call rendered him as helpless as a child, he was hardly the last player to experience such a youthful feeling at the Midsummer Classic. Four years later, Larry Walker came to the plate against Johnson and batted righty for the first time in his career, wearing his batting helmet backward. Thankfully for Walker, another lasting All-Star memory was one of wonder rather than terror. After playing in the 1999 Midsummer Classic at Fenway Park — one that saw members of baseball's All-Century Team convene in Boston — Walker was so awestruck by his historic surroundings that he couldn't help but snag a souvenir.

"I hope the grounds crew doesn't get too mad, because I tore this piece of grass out of right field," Walker said, displaying the chunk of green sod to reporters. "I'm taking it home and I'm going to have it forever."

LOOK OUT ABOVE
The NL's John Kruk
cowered through an
at-bat against Randy
Johnson after an errant
pitch in the '93 game.

LAWN CARE

The All-Star Game is all about the details. It's not just a coincidence, then, that everything in the ballpark on game day is designed to showcase baseball's top talent, even down to the blades of grass.

MLB groundskeepers have become increasingly creative in dressing up the grass for the Midsummer Classic. In addition to using the All-Star Game logo, which is painted onto the field in foul territory, each host team's grounds crew has decorated the field in unique ways. "Grass is the perfect canvas, and patterns are only limited by your imagination," said David Mellor, director of grounds for the Boston Red Sox, who hosted the game in 1999.

But the design can't interfere with the game, either. "I don't want to see a bad hop," said Mellor. "Safety and playability are the first priority."

In 2007, San Francisco's grounds crew adorned the outfield grass for part of its All-Star Week events with the image of a ball splashing into the bay — an element of the game's logo that year, which represented a home run landing in McCovey Cove just outside AT&T Park's walls.

Groundskeepers at Angel Stadium took similar liberty with the outfield grass during 2010's All-Star festivities, mowing a star pattern topped with a halo into center field. And a year earlier, Busch Stadium depicted St. Louis's signature Gateway Arch in its expansive outfield. The craftsmanship of the arch — stretching from the foul line just behind third base to the foul line just behind first — emulated the monument itself, which is visible in the city skyline beyond the stadium. The team liked the design so much that, since the 2009 game, it has been used repeatedly on the field.

"The ultimate home run is a situation like in St. Louis," said Anne Occi, MLB's vice president of design services. "They are still mowing the arch into the grass today, years after it was done for the All-Star Game."

WHICH WAY THE WIND BLOWS

A pitcher named to an All-Star team generally has a reputation for blowing away hitters. But in one very memorable incident, it was a pitcher himself who was blown away during the Midsummer Classic.

The 1961 game in San Francisco was a 10-inning thriller, but it's remembered most for Giants pitcher Stu Miller being blown off the mound. Miller replaced Sandy Koufax with the NL holding a 3-2 lead in the ninth. "I was used to the wind, so I anchored myself after I came to my stretch position," Miller said. "An extra gust of wind rocked me back and forth, just a couple of inches. But it was enough." The umpires called a balk after the pitch.

Aside from Miller's missteps, the elements have been kinder for other Midsummer Classics. Dubbed that for a reason, temperatures are balmy more often than not, and no games have been cancelled due to inclement weather.

GATEWAY TO THE WEST
Groundskeepers mirrored the Gateway Arch for the '09 contest at Busch Stadium.

SUDDEN IMPACT

QUICK SUCCESS IN THE MAJORS IS RARE, AND THREE MONTHS is barely enough time for a rookie to establish a reputation. But every so often, a first-year player does enough to get the All-Star call.

Joe DiMaggio entered the 1936 All-Star Game as the first freshman ever voted into the lineup. But the game was a disaster for the 21-year-old, whom the *Los Angeles Times* proclaimed "the unanimous selection for All-American goat." He misjudged a fly ball, allowing an RBI triple, then misplayed a single for an error. He also made the game's final out to cap an awful 0-for-5 day.

No rookie pitcher started the All-Star Game until 1962, when Dave Stenhouse, a 28-year-old engineer and former Army lieutenant, set the AL on its ear. Almost two decades later, in 1981, the most remarkable rookie All-Star — the Dodgers' Fernando Valenzuela — held the baseball universe in the palm of his hand. Using a devastating screwball, the 20-year-old won his first eight starts, including an Opening Day outing, tossing nine innings in each with a 0.50 ERA.

When Tony Oliva cracked the 1964 AL starting lineup, he wasn't just challenged by Big League pitchers, but also by a new culture and language. But Oliva was fluent at the plate. He bashed AL pitching during the '64 season, becoming the first rookie to win a batting title. But he, too, struggled in his All-Star debut, going 0 for 4.

With a 9-2 record and a 1.78 ERA for the Tigers, Mark Fidrych earned the start for the AL in the 1976 All-Star Game. Despite the promising start, the idiosyncratic ex–gas station attendant injured his pitching arm and won just 10 more games after his rookie season.

Maturity would characterize a newer breed of rookie All-Stars, as teams tapped into the Asian talent pool. In 1995, the first Japan-born Big Leaguer in three decades, Hideo Nomo, became the biggest rookie pitching sensation since fellow Dodger Valenzuela. With his 6-1 record and 1.99 ERA at the break, Nomo was named the NL's starting pitcher. A similar frenzy followed Ichiro Suzuki, MLB's first Japanese position player, in 2001. After leading all players in All-Star voting, he went 1 for 3 with a steal in the Midsummer Classic.

In 2010, Braves freshman sensation Jason Heyward earned a starting spot in the contest even though an injury kept him from participating. "It's my first time experiencing it. There are other guys here that are older than me and it's their first time, but still, you're just taking it all in," he said during the game.

J-HEY-KID
Braves rookie Jason Heyward was a first-time All-Star in 2010.

FIRST OF HIS KIND
The Yankees' Joe DiMaggio (left), shown with NL All-Star Dizzy Dean, was the first rookie ever voted to an All-Star team, in 1936.

NO PLACE LIKE HOME

WHILE CITIES BEGIN PREPARING FAR IN ADVANCE TO HOST the All-Star Game, players representing the home team are often asked to do their part on short notice. As the National League manager in 2006, Phil Garner saw firsthand what Pirates All-Stars Jason Bay and Freddy Sanchez faced when the game came to Pittsburgh. "There's a lot of attention for those guys that play here. There's just no time to gather your thoughts."

"Getting to play in front of the fans in Pittsburgh," Sanchez said after receiving a surprising 800,000-plus votes as a write-in candidate on the ballot, "is an honor."

Just as players yearn for the chance to take the All-Star stage at home, fans thrive on seeing their local boys. Ten Yankees were in uniform for the first Midsummer Classic in the Bronx in 1939. And that was before fan voting was instituted. Now, as All-Star excitement builds in the host city, fans have been known to vote feverishly to ensure that the home team is well represented. Bay and Sanchez both benefited from a last-minute voting surge in Pittsburgh; the efforts paid off particularly well for Bay, who was elected to start. "It took a lot of effort by a lot of people," Bay said.

Giving fans a glimpse of their local heroes in action — not merely just in uniform — is essential, too. When Red Schoendienst managed the 1968 Senior Circuit squad, he saw to it that Houston's Rusty Staub, a reserve in the game, got a pinch-hit at-bat in front of the Astrodome crowd.

Bob Brenly represented the Giants in '84, when the Midsummer Classic was played at San Francisco's Candlestick Park. "It was unbelievable," said Brenly, now a Cubs broadcaster. "Reggie Smith [a hometown star with the Dodgers in 1980] and some of the other veterans said, 'You will never get an ovation like you get from your home crowd at an All-Star Game.' They didn't lie. It sent chills up and down my spine."

When the All-Star Game came to Anaheim in 2010, the Angels' Torii Hunter and Jered Weaver were heralded by a home fan base, as well. The honor was doubly sentimental for Weaver, as he played not only in his home stadium but also in his hometown. For Hunter, it was a thrill to be a part of the game in the friendly center-field confines. "It's awesome to go out there and represent the Angels and all the fans," Hunter said. "This is my home turf!"

> "It was unbelievable. Reggie Smith and some of the other veterans said, 'You will never get an ovation like you get from your home crowd at an All-Star Game.' They didn't lie. It sent chills up and down my spine." —Bob Brenly

AMBASSADORS

SOME OF THE GAME'S MOST ESTEEMED PLAYERS — PAST AND present — are chosen to serve as ambassadors when the game rolls into their teams' cities.

St. Louis's Midsummer Classic fever peaked in 2009, when the city hosted the contest and saw its slugging hero, Albert Pujols, heavily promote the festivities before taking the field at Busch Stadium. Mingling with Cardinals greats, fielding questions from the media and catching President Barack Obama's ceremonial first pitch, Pujols ushered in the game in grand fashion. And the Angels' Torii Hunter took notice. He was an ambassador — along with club legend Rod Carew — for the 2010 game and its five-day All-

Star FanFest in Anaheim. "That's the kind of the warm welcome you want when you're hosting the All-Star Game," Hunter said. "It's something I'll never forget and the fans here will never forget."

Luis Gonzalez saw to it that the All-Star Game was greeted with the appropriate amount of pomp and circumstance when the game made its way to Arizona in 2011. A five-time All-Star and 2001 World Series hero with the D-backs, Gonzalez was involved in a series of MLB activities leading up to All-Star Week in July 2011 at Chase Field. "I spent the best years of my career in Phoenix with the Diamondbacks," Gonzalez said, "and being involved in the first Midsummer Classic here is very special."

HEAVEN SENT
Hall of Famer Rod
Carew (left) and
2010 All-Star Torii
Hunter welcomed
the Midsummer
Classic to Anaheim.

MAN OF THE HOUR One Stan Musial (scoring) swing launched the homer that capped a 12-inning NL win in 1955.

MEN IN BLUE

THIRTY-FOUR PLAYERS REPRESENT EACH LEAGUE DURING THE All-Star Game. But there are six spots on the field that won't be filled by players come game day — they're reserved for the men in blue.

Of MLB's 68 umpires, only a half-dozen are chosen to work the All-Star Game each year. According to Randy Marsh, MLB's director of umpiring, the representatives are picked based on their performance in the first half of the season. Seniority also factors into the decision, and one crew chief is tabbed. Positions are based on tenure, too, as the most senior umpire calls balls and strikes.

Former umpire Mike Reilly, a 34-season vet, got that job twice. "You always, in your career, want to work home plate in an All-Star Game before you retire," said Reilly, who had the honor in 2000 and again in 2010 before retiring at season's end. "I have my shirt that I wore in that game — it's in a frame now in my office."

MLB's baseball operations department and umpire supervisors determine who officiates the All-Star Game. When circumstances permit, there will be special consideration given to a qualified candidate that has local ties to the game, as was the case when Michigan native Tim Welke umpired first base at Comerica Park in '05.

The All-Star Game may have a jubilant atmosphere, but umpires cannot relax, especially since Commissioner Bud Selig offered home-field advantage in the World Series to the winning league.

"The fact that the game meant something, I think it put more pressure on the umpires to perform at a high level because of what was at stake for the players," Reilly said. "So instead of being a celebration game, you could see the intensity on the field."

But it's not all work, either. Many umpires bring their families to the game and take part in plenty of All-Star Week festivities.

LATE DRAMA

OVER THE LAST 75 YEARS, LAST-GASP MIDSUMMER CLASSIC heroics have provided the sport with some of its most dramatic moments, from walk-off shots by legends to violent collisions that have altered careers and reputations.

Although he wasn't known as a showman in the vein of Babe Ruth, NL representative Stan Musial did take a cue from the Bambino in the 1955 All-Star Game in Milwaukee, calling his shot on a dramatic home run — he just preferred to do it more subtly. When Stan "the Man" came to the plate with the score tied in the 12th, he inquired of AL catcher Yogi Berra, "How ya doing, Yogi?" Berra replied that the extra innings were killing his feet. Retorted Musial, "Don't worry, I'll get us out of here in a hurry." And he did, launching the first pitch he saw into County Stadium's right-field bleachers. Hank Aaron, then a 21-year-old in his first Midsummer Classic, also witnessed Musial's called shot. "I remember him standing up and saying, 'They don't pay us to play overtime.' And he went up and hit a home run."

High drama also appeared on the All-Star stage in 1950, when the NL ended a run of futility thanks to clutch home runs from future Hall of Famers Ralph Kiner and Red Schoendienst. With his team trailing, 3-2, Kiner launched a solo shot into the left-field bleachers at Chicago's Comiskey Park to send the game into extra innings. Schoendienst, a defensive specialist who had just 14 career home runs at the time, then stepped to the plate to lead off the top of the 14th. He reportedly told his teammates, "I'm going up there

and parking one in the left-field stands." On a 2-2 pitch, he did just that to give the NL a 4-3 victory.

The 1970 contest in Cincinnati brought exhibition-game drama to an entirely new — and controversial — level. With the game locked in the bottom of the 12th, host club star Pete Rose was so determined to score the winning run that he collided with AL catcher Ray Fosse, sending him sprawling.

As the first All-Star Game to determine World Series home-field advantage, the 2003 contest was marketed with the slogan "This Time It Counts." It was a good thing for Dodgers closer Eric Gagne that it didn't count in the stat sheet, though. Facing Texas's Hank Blalock in the eighth, Gagne served up a pitch that Blalock launched for a mammoth two-run bomb, turning the NL's one-run lead into a one-run deficit, the only blown save for Gagne in a 22-month period.

After nine consecutive winless efforts, it seemed as if the NL was going to break through in 2006. Having taken a one-run lead thanks to dominant pitching, clever baserunning and a homer off the bat of David Wright, the NL handed its fate to Padres closer Trevor Hoffman. The 38-year-old legend made short work of the first two AL batters, but then gave up two straight hits. And after registering two quick strikes on the Rangers' Michael Young, Hoffman threw a fastball that caught too much of the plate, and the 29-year-old shortstop took it the other way for a triple. The hit gave the AL a 3-2 lead that closer Mariano Rivera would preserve in the bottom of the ninth.

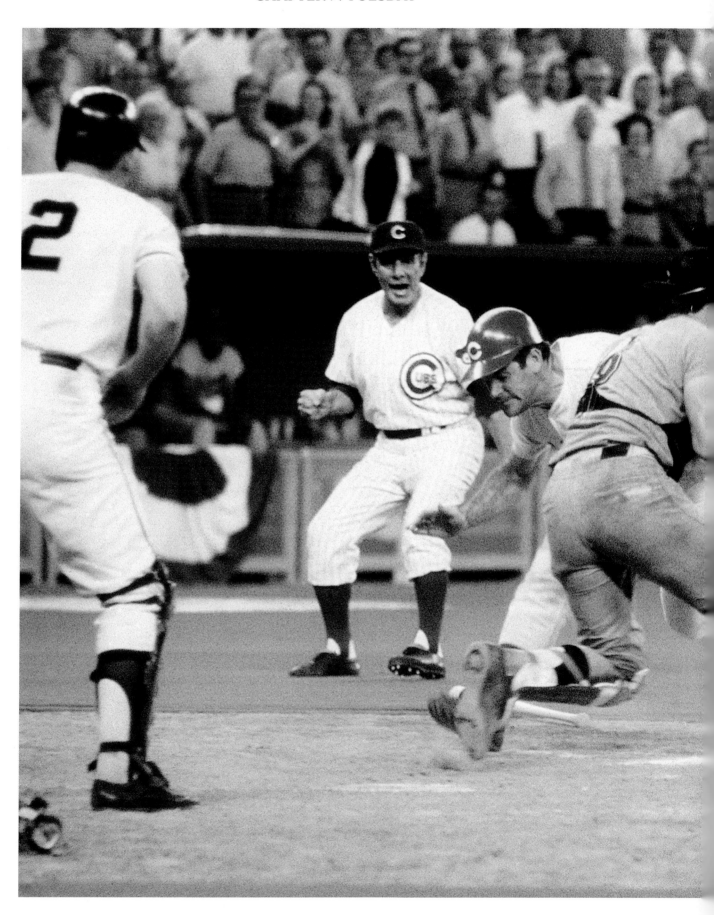

CRASH COURSE
Pete Rose didn't let Ray Fosse block his way to the plate with the game on the line in the 1970 All-Star Game.

AUTHENTICATION

FOR MANY BASEBALL ENTHUSIASTS, ONE OF THE JOYS OF ALL-STAR WEEK IS THE COLLECTION of memorabilia. And a group of 16 independent third-party authenticators is charged with making sure that fans looking for Midsummer Classic collectibles are getting the real deal. From the autograph tables at All-Star FanFest to the field during the State Farm Home Run Derby, the authenticators record and place an identifying hologram on items such as jerseys, broken bats and more.

To ensure authenticity, Michael Posner and Howard Shelton, managers of the MLB authentication program, and the authenticators must cover a lot of ground during All-Star Week. They're often in the clubhouse autograph rooms, where players can get items signed by teammates. First-timers certainly frequent the rooms, and Ichiro Suzuki is a regular, too. Authenticators observe and tag each signed item, but occasionally things get more interesting. In 2010, Josh Hamilton walked into the clubhouse after leaving the game, took off his uniform, and had it, as well as his glove and bats from the game, authenticated.

The Home Run Derby is the only event for which the authenticators are actually on the field. If you looked closely in Anaheim in 2010, you could have spotted an authenticator on the rock pile in left-center field, waiting to authenticate home run balls.

"What's great about baseball is the rich history," said Posner. "Fans and players alike are always looking to own a piece of history and we work to make sure that what they have is genuine."

Authenticators also put their seal on a charitable initiative in 2010, as they watched every All-Star sign a copy of the *Major League Baseball Opus*, an 850-page book detailing the history of the game. The signed copy was auctioned, with the proceeds going to the RBI program and the Players' Trust.

After All-Star Week, authenticated items are securely shipped back to Major League Baseball's Park Avenue office in New York. The 2010 shipment contained some 100 boxes and included everything from players' locker tags to dirt from the mound and home plate.

INKED UP The signatures of players, like Jered Weaver, are authenticated in autograph rooms.

HARDWARE

ONE OF THE MOST MEMORABLE MOMENTS IN ALL-STAR GAME HISTORY CAME BEFORE THE 1999 contest at Fenway Park, when Ted Williams was honored as part of the All-Century Team. In 2002, baseball found another more enduring way to recognize the "Splendid Splinter," renaming the game's MVP trophy the Ted Williams MVP Award after the legend who died just four days before that year's Midsummer Classic.

When the honor debuted at the 1962 All-Star Game, the trophy was dubbed the Arch Ward Memorial Award in honor of the late sports editor credited with dreaming up the All-Star Game. Renamed the Commissioner's Trophy in 1970, the original moniker was restored when the prize awarded to the World Series champion assumed the latter title. Ward's namesake stuck until Williams' passing. In a unique twist, the first recipient of the Ted Williams MVP Award didn't come until 2003, a year after its debut, because the 2002 Midsummer Classic ended in a tie. Angels outfielder Garret Anderson snagged the honor in '03, powering the AL to victory.

As with the name, the design of the trophy has changed over the years. When the Rangers' Michael Young received the trophy for his performance in 2006, the award resembled a three-dimensional crystal star. "This is a pretty big highlight in my baseball career," Young said. "I think everyone dreams of having a big All-Star Game. Even coming to the All-Star Game is humbling enough, but to be in this situation now where I have an All-Star Game MVP Award is pretty exciting."

Since 2009, the trophy has been a crystal replica of a regulation-size bat, stretching 34 inches in length. Valued at more than $9,000, it is created by Steuben, the company's preeminent crystal maker since 1903. Each piece of Steuben is handmade using a variety of artisanal techniques that only a few extraordinary craftsmen are able to master. Rays outfielder Carl Crawford took home the first crystal bat in St. Louis, and Brian McCann received it the next season after ending the NL's 13-year drought.

CRYSTAL SLUGGER Commissioner Bud Selig (left) honored Brian McCann as the 2010 All-Star MVP.

SOURCE NOTES

CHAPTER 1

13: Dutton, Bob. "Baseball's All-Star Game returning to KC in 2012." *The Kansas City Star.* June 17, 2010. A1.

13: Gutierrez, Paul. "Getting the game not as easy as it appears." *The Sacramento Bee.* July 3, 2007. C1.

13: Kaegel, Dick. "Royals tabbed to host 2012 All-Star Game." MLB.com. June 16, 2010.

16: Gilbert, Steve. "D-backs thrilled with All-Star Game logo." MLB.com. Dec. 15, 2010.

17: Drebinger, John. "American League Beats Rivals, 4-2." *The New York Times.* July 7, 1933.

17: Freedman, Lew. *The Day All the Stars Came Out, 1933.* Jefferson, NC: McFarland, 2010.

17: "M'Graw Congratulates Victorious Team; Calls Ruth's Deeds in Battle Marvelous." *The New York Times.* July 7, 1933.

17: Vincent, David, Lyle Spatz, and David W. Smith. *The Midsummer Classic: The Complete History of Baseball's All-Star Game.* Lincoln, NE: Bison Books, 2001.

17: Macgranachan, Brendan. "Addie Joss' Benefit Game." Seamheads.com, July 25, 2009.

17: "Pitcher Joss Dead, Ill Only Few Days." *The New York Times.* April 15, 1911.

17: Untitled game summary. *The New York Times.* July 25, 1911.

20–21: Lester, Larry. *Black Baseball's National Showcase: The East-West All-Star Game, 1933-1953.* Lincoln, NE: Bison Books, 2002.

22: Brown, Maury. "Inside Planning the MLB All-Star Game." *The Biz of Baseball.* July 12, 2010.

22: Kennelly, Lisa. "Cranford's Occi does more than 'patch' work." *The Star-Ledger.* July 21, 2008. 37.

22: Stone, Larry. "All-Star cast goes to work." *The Seattle Times.* July 9, 2000. D11.

CHAPTER 2

34: Nightengale, Bob. "Due Process." *Official MLB 2006 All-Star Game Program.* July 11, 2006. 27.

40–41: Drebinger, John. "American League Beats Rivals, 4-2." *The New York Times.* July 7, 1933.

40–41: Kieran, John. "Excitement in All Directions." *The New York Times.* July 6, 1933.

40–41: "M'Graw Congratulates Victorious Team; Calls Ruth's Deeds in Battle Marvelous." *The New York Times.* July 7, 1933.

40–41: Ritter, Lawrence S. *The Glory of Their Times.* New York: Harper Paperbacks. 1992.

42: Jones, David. "Stellar Starts." *Official MLB 2005 All-Star Game Program.* July 12, 2005. 86.

43: Schwarz, Alan. "Thanks, Hank." *Official MLB 2003 World Series Program.* October 2003. 34.

CHAPTER 3

50: Rutter, Joe. "Minor-league game offers glimpse into future." *Pittsburgh Tribune-Review.* July 6, 2006.

53: Greenberg, Chris. "Looking Ahead." *Official MLB 2009 All-Star Game Program.* July 14, 2009. 34.

54: Newhan, Ross. "New in Blue." *Los Angeles Times.* July 7, 1998.

54: Mitchell, Fred. "Whitaker is Short One Shirt." *Chicago Tribune.* July 17, 1985.

60: Newman, Mark. "All-Star Fun Run raises money, awareness." MLB.com. July 11, 2010.

64: Davis, Rick. "Program drives home baseball, life lessons for local youths." *The San Diego Union-Tribune.* July 10, 2010. D-7.

CHAPTER 5

90–95: Stark, Jayson. "Hit It Here." *Official MLB 2007 All-Star Game Program.* July 10, 2007. 70.

96: Enders, Eric. "Outta Here!" *Official MLB 2010 All-Star Game Program.* July 13, 2010. 78.

99: Hurdle, Clint and Schwartz, Jon. "The Accidental Spotlight." *Official MLB 2010 All-Star Game Program.* July 13, 2010. 62.

104: Calkins, Matt. "All-Star Pitch." *The Press Enterprise.* July 10, 2010. A1.

CHAPTER 6

111: Farmer, Sam. "Fantasy Meets Reality." *Los Angeles Times.* July 10, 2010. C3.

111: Hutchinson, Bill. "That ball is … Here!" *Daily News.* July 6, 2008. 20.

111: Phillips, Michael. "Pirates Fans Enjoy Preview of FanFest." *Pittsburgh Post-Gazette.* June 14, 2006. F-5.

117: Hodge, Shelby. "Party Scene." *The Houston Chronicle.* July 13, 2004. 9.

118: Cohen, Rachel. "More than 40 baseball Hall of Famers committed to attend MLB All-Star pregame ceremony." The Associated Press. June 4, 2008.

124: Brown, Maury. "Musical Talent for 2010 All-Star Game Events Features 'Glee' Cast Member, Rock Band 'Train.'" *The Biz of Baseball.* July 11, 2010.

126: Schwartz, Jon. "The Thinker." *Official MLB 2007 All-Star Game Program.* July 10, 2007. 199.

128: Hiestand, Michael. "Obama may get more than All-Star pitch." Gannett News Service. July 21, 2009.

CHAPTER 7

132: Appel, Marty. "23 Innings of Baseball Heaven." *Official MLB 2003 All-Star Game Program.* July 15, 2003. 47.

134: Woodcock, Les. "The Greatest Shows on Earth." *Official MLB 2000 All-Star Game Program.* July 11, 2000. 57.

135: Crasnick, Jerry. "A Midsummer Night's Streak." *Official MLB 2010 All-Star Game Program.* July 13, 2010. 43.

135: Maciborski, Nathan. "Midsummer Dreamin'." *Official MLB 2008 All-Star Game Program.* July 15, 2008. 62.

137: Doyle, Paul. "Broadway Stage." *Hartford Courant.* July 13, 2008. E5.

137: Maciborski, Nathan. "A Red Carpet Ride." *Official MLB 2007 All-Star Game Program.* July 10, 2007. 31.

140: Bush, David. "No Signal." *Official MLB 2007 All-Star Game Program.* July 10, 2007. 37.

142: Enders, Eric. "Classic Duels." *Official MLB 2005 All-Star Game Program.* July 12, 2005. 51.

144: Bush, David. "Hold On To Your Hats." *Official MLB 2007 All-Star Game Program.* July 10, 2007. 200.

146: Enders, Eric. "Sudden Impacts." *Official MLB 2006 All-Star Game Program.* July 11, 2006. 46.

148: Krest, Shawn. "Home Cooking." *Official MLB 2007 All-Star Game Program.* July 10, 2007. 56.

148: Gilbert, Steve. "Gonzalez named All-Star Game ambassador." MLB.com. Jan. 24, 2011.

151: Jones, David. "Final Act." *Official MLB 2007 All-Star Game Program.* July 10, 2007. 48.

154: Glier, Ray. "Players take collectibles, memories." *The Atlanta Journal-Constitution.* July 13, 2010. 1C.

CREDITS

MICHAEL BUCKNER/GETTY IMAGES: Front Cover; 55; 132–133

RICH PILLING/MLB PHOTOS: Back Cover (FanFest Ball, Hawpe); 2–3; 8; 10; 12; 23; 24–25; 26; 29; 32; 35; 45; 50–51; 58–59; 60–61; 62–63; 70; 78–79; 88; 90; 91; 92–93; 94–95; 95; 107; 108; 110; 112–113; 114–115; 120; 125; 126–127; 130; 132–133; 146; 149; 154; 155

DAVID LILIENSTEIN/MLB PHOTOS: Back Cover (Red Carpet); 106; 136

NICK LAHAM/GETTY IMAGES: Back Cover (Tickets); 30

JESSICA FOSTER/MLB PHOTOS: 5; 138; 144–145

JEFF GROSS/GETTY IMAGES: 6; 100–101; 119

TIM UMPHREY/GETTY IMAGES: 14–15

MARK RUCKER/TRANSCENDENTAL GRAPHICS/GETTY IMAGES: 18–19; 20–21; 47; 147; 150

NBLA/MLB PHOTOS: 40–41

JEFF ZELEVANSKY/MLB PHOTOS: 27

RONALD MARTINEZ/GETTY IMAGES: 28

MATT BROWN/MLB PHOTOS: 36; 38–39; 86–87; 103

ALLEN KEE/MLB PHOTOS: 43; 124

JOE ANGELES/MLB PHOTOS: 48

STEPHEN DUNN/GETTY IMAGES: 52

BRIAN BAHR/GETTY IMAGES: 56–57

DAVID ALTMAN/MLB PHOTOS: 65

JED JACOBSOHN/GETTY IMAGES: 66

RICK STEWART/GETTY IMAGES: 69; 140–141

PETE SOUZA/THE WHITE HOUSE/GETTY IMAGES: 72–73

MARC LEVINE/MLB PHOTOS: 74

DILIP VISHWANAT/GETTY IMAGES: 80–81

AL BELLO/GETTY IMAGES: 82–83

BRUCE BENNETT/GETTY IMAGES: 97

MARK CUNNINGHAM/MLB PHOTOS: 98

BOB ROSATO/MLB PHOTOS: 99

JAMIE SQUIRE/GETTY IMAGES: 105

STEPHEN JAFFE/AFP/GETTY IMAGES: 121

EZRA O. SHAW/GETTY IMAGES: 122–123

MLB PHOTOS: 116–117; 129; 143

JOHN MABANGLO/AFP/GETTY IMAGES: 134

CHRISTIAN PETERSEN/GETTY IMAGES: 137; 139

HERB SCHARFMAN/SPORTS IMAGERY/GETTY IMAGES: 152–153

INDEX

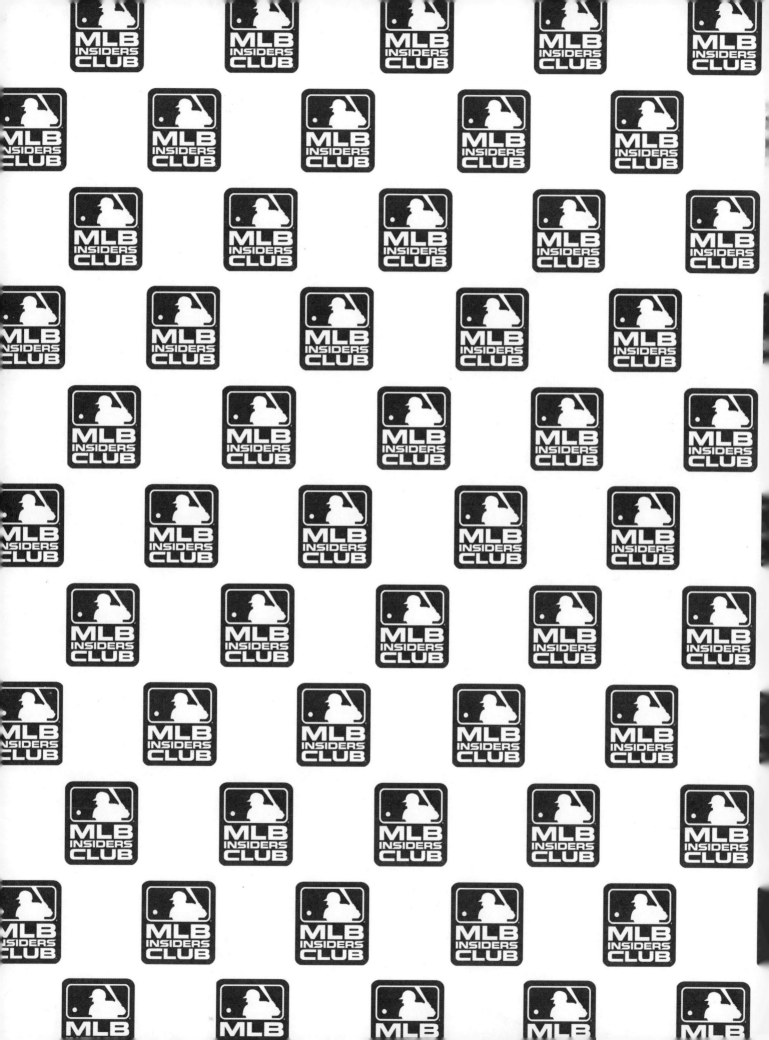